STRONG ENOUGH FOR TWO

Women Taking the Strain in a Relationship

Liz Roberts

Piccadilly Press · London

Acknowledgements:

To all at No 52, Paultons Square for their patience
and support and to Dr Guy O'Keefe for general
medical advice.

Phototypeset by Goodfellow & Egan, Cambridge
Printed and bound in Great Britain by
Biddles Ltd, Guildford and King's Lynn
for the publishers, Piccadilly Press Ltd,
5 Castle Road, London NW1 8PR

A catalogue record for this book is available from the
British Library

ISBN 1-85340-245-1

Liz Roberts author of many successful books, is a former
Sunday Times journalist who now works freelance. This is her
first book for Piccadilly Press.

CONTENTS

Introduction

INTRODUCTION

This book is written for women who find themselves having to take the strain in a relationship. "For better" has become "for worse". There are many reasons why a man may cease to be a shoulder to lean on, and become the one who needs support. Redundancy, business failure, a breakdown in health, drug or alcohol addiction – any of these can trigger a dramatic increase in your responsibilities.

There are no "right" or "wrong" answers to life's crises. You are faced with choices, and ultimately it is up to you to decide which path to take. This book will help you develop ways of coping with situations, to act constructively and not just dwell on "why me?". And when you have dealt with immediate problems there will be hard thinking to do about the future. Do you want to stay together? What about the children?

It might be some consolation to know that others have suffered a fate similar to your own. You may also find help and guidance in reading about other people's experiences. And there are lots of suggestions about organisations to consult and practical steps to take that may be right for you.

ADDICTION

Part One

ADDICTION

1. DRINK

THE FAMILY DISEASE

Problem drinking – alcoholism – is often called "the family disease". This is because the problems involved with obsessive drinking inevitably spill over into the lives of the drinker's partner and children. Excessive drinking may be perceived as the "norm" and more than one generation can be affected as patterns of behaviour are learned within families and passed on. There may even be a genetic element to alcoholism. Partners and children not only have to cope with difficult behaviour but are also called upon for support and help.

"My father was a drunk from a family riddled for generations by alcoholism. His wild bingeing lost him one job after another until finally he sat in the house all day, drinking and feeling inadequate, fantasizing that my mother was seeing other men.

3

He blacked her eyes regularly. Nobody in my family spoke. We all screamed. We all screamed at each other at the top of our voices. When the police came, everyone knew my father had threatened to kill my mother again."
(Pat, quoted by Nan Robertson in *Getting Better – Inside Alcoholics Anonymous,* Macmillan, 1988)

"My post-doctoral fellowship required that I study one chronic disease in depth. I chose alcoholism. I read as much as I could and in due time proposed to my departmental chairman that I present a lecture on alcoholism. I invited a psychiatrist . . . in the few minutes preceding the lectures I heard him say, 'Oh, several members of my family are alcoholics'. I froze. I felt panic. It took me nearly a month to understand what had happened to me. He had given voice to something I had long repressed. I came to recognise that alcoholism existed in my family. This person's honesty had broken what I considered a taboo, a family secret."
(Ken, 38, doctor, from *Al-Anon Sharings from Adult Children*)

MISCONCEPTIONS OF ALCOHOLISM

People with drink problems do not necessarily look like tramps or reel about in the streets waving bottles. They might just drink quietly and steadily every night at home without necessarily showing that they are drunk.

"My father used to drink all evening, then go to bed. We only realised he was an alcoholic when he was taken ill and the doctor said he had cirrhosis of the liver from years of excessive alcohol intake."
(Miranda, 32, housewife)

"Drinkers get very good at concealment and manipulation. I didn't realise how much my husband was drinking because he was so good at hiding it. Of course, when I look back, I can see the little things he did, such as inventing extra work which gave him an excuse to be out of the house and get back 'tired' (i.e. drunk)."
(Jenny, 41, office manager)

Many alcoholics manage to achieve success in their work – lawyers, actors, writers, politicians and diplomats have many problem drinkers in their ranks. A recent table highlighting the occupational risk of alcoholism showed that people commercially involved with drink – publicans, waiters, barmen and hotel managers – are in the highest categories. Doctors are surprisingly high in the table too. Officers in the armed forces and (amazingly) pilots and air flight controllers also figure on the list.

Studies suggest that any combination of: easy access to liquor, poor pay, job-related stress, and unsocial hours are the main factors responsible for making these occupations high risk as far as problem drinking is concerned. The most recent estimate shows that as many as 14 million working days a year are lost to British industry due to the after-effects of drink. The problem is so common and involves so many people that, ironically, the partners of problem drinkers get little sympathy or support from some medical advisers or bosses when they try to discuss their worries.

"I finally gave up trying to enlist the support of my husband's employers in his drinking problem. They didn't want to know – to them, it looked as though I was the problem, not him – even though he had let them down repeatedly through being drunk, crashing the company car and so on."
(Sybil, 50, sales assistant)

WHEN IS IT "PROBLEM DRINKING"?

Signs that your partner is not in control of his alcohol consumption include:

- persistent trouble getting up in the morning because of previous night's drinking

Addiction – Drink

- rows about drink
- money problems because of excessive drinking
- secret drinking
- drinking earlier and earlier in the day
- physical problems such as "the shakes"
- loss of memory, including "blackouts" and "blank pages"
- violence when drunk

"He would come in and I would be all tensed up, worried sick, and angry and we would immediately start a quarrel which then deteriorated into him threatening me with violence. Sometimes the threat alone, him looming over me in this half-crazed state was worse than actually being lashed out at. I thought to myself: he's going to kill me, he's going to kill me."
(Jenny)

"It wasn't difficult for him to hide how much he was drinking because he worked in the restaurant business. At Chinese New Year, for instance, he gave a party for all his Chinese staff and each person at the table had a whole bottle of whisky set at their place. Excessive drinking was the norm, I would say. He would get up late and have a beer and go out and have a boozy lunch, go on to a drinking club in the West End and from there have a meal, more drink and then stay at a night-club he managed until the

early hours. He always had a glass of white wine or whisky to hand – never being sick or falling over, but just drunk all day long."
(Millie, 36, antique dealer)

Doctors label certain types of problem drinkers "dependent" or "addictive" personalities. This means that they look for solutions to their difficulties outside themselves. Drink controls them, rather than vice versa. Eventually the whole of a person's body is geared to getting nourishment from alcohol rather than other protein. Weaning off is a painful process involving physical withdrawal symptoms similar to those described by heroin addicts.

Positive Steps You Can Take

If a problem drinker wants and seeks help, there is plenty that can be done. However, whether or not your partner seeks help, it is up to you to break the cycle of powerlessness by taking control of your own life. You also need to acknowledge that the help you alone can give an alcoholic is limited.

Here are some of the things that you can and should do once the problem is recognised:

A) SEEK OUT INFORMATION

A good place to start is Al-Anon, the organisation for relatives and friends of alcoholics. It has first-hand experience and understanding of the plight of the alcoholic. It is not a professional counselling organisation but does publish many helpful leaflets.

Al-Anon family groups gather together to share their experience, and a great deal of relief is gained from discussing and recognising standard problems. You no longer feel alone. Even greater relief is gained from hearing genuinely helpful tips to enable everyone involved to regain control over their lives.

"I just went and sat at meetings and cried and cried and cried. Then I began to be able to listen to what other people were saying, and I began to think: 'I'll hang on to that.' It's important for a person to let go of that fear – you know, 'what happens if . . .' You have to learn to let go and let God, as they say in Al-Anon."
(Pauline, 41, counsellor)

Al-Anon offers a list of points that many have found helpful:

- Learn all the facts and put them to work in your own life. Don't start with the alcoholic.
- Attend group therapy meetings, a mental health

clinic, and an alcoholism centre. Get competent counselling or visit a minister with experience in this field.

- Remember you are emotionally involved. Changing your attitude and approach to the problem can speed up recovery
- Encourage all activities beneficial to the alcoholic and cooperate in making them possible
- Learn that love cannot exist without compassion, discipline and justice, and to accept or give love without these qualities is to destroy it eventually
- Don't lecture, moralise, scold, blame, threaten, argue, pour out liquor, lose your temper or cover up the consequences of drinking. You may feel better, but the situation will be worse
- Don't allow your anxiety to compel you to do for alcoholics what they must do for themselves
- Don't accept promises, for this is just a method of postponing pain. In the same way, don't keep switching agreements. If an agreement is made, stick to it
- Don't knowingly accept a lie for the truth for in so doing you encourage this habit. The truth is often painful, but get at it
- Don't let the alcoholic outsmart you for this teaches him or her to avoid responsibility and lose respect for you at the same time

"It's tough, breaking the habits of a lifetime. You

must have people you can confide in, and to back you up – it is a tall order keeping everything straight in your head without that support behind you."
(Susie, 32, office worker)

Another London-based organisation, ACCEPT, runs groups for families and friends of problem drinkers led by an experienced person they call "a facilitator".

"We are encouraged to understand what kind of people we are – that is, the partners of problem drinkers. It's quite interesting to discover how many of us had a problem-drinker parent. Going to the group gives me support. We are encouraged to look at our own choices, instead of blaming everything on our partner. We don't have to stay, we don't have to accept the drinking, they call it taking back power for yourself. You should never say: 'If only he would change', You have the power – it's as simple (and difficult!) as that."
(Susie)

B) RECOGNISE YOUR ROLE IN THE PROBLEM

Although it is your partner who is the alcoholic you – unwittingly – may be the cause of many of the family problems. For instance, it is a natural reaction to deny that anything is wrong, at least to the

11

outside world, and sometimes even to yourself. Unfortunately the result of denial is that your partner is even less in control of his life if you are constantly minimising and hiding the damage caused by his drunken behaviour. Vomit or urine on carpets is "tidied up". Absences from work due to drink are "explained away". You may feel obliged to keep your partner company at all times to prevent him from drinking. Often the rest of the family take on the responsibility for the alcoholic's life.

"Help" of this nature may in fact prevent your partner from gaining genuine self-esteem through personal achievement. You should beware of inadvertently undermining fragile self-confidence. It is important to be able to take responsibility for your own life and recognise the limits of responsibility for another's.

"I stopped fighting it and covering up and worrying. It took time to get used to, and sometimes I failed. But things start to get better almost right away when you put 'letting go' into practice."
(Pauline)

C) LETTING GO/TOUGH LOVE
It is difficult to love and accept other people without loving and accepting yourself. Being on forgiving terms with yourself "warts and all" is a prerequisite for being able to forgive. *You* are important. You

shouldn't deny yourself in order to love someone else, or feel that love is detrimental to your own needs.

"My first reaction was: it's not me, it's him. The turning point is building up your own self-esteem – accepting other people for what they are."
(Susie)

"I never seemed to put myself first. I don't know when the habit started – it may even have been before I married. But it was a great struggle for me to begin to think about my own priorities rather than his. It was amazing how that helped the atmosphere – I felt that at least I was getting somewhere, and that made things easier all round."
(Sybil)

"I needed to separate myself out from the situation – see myself as a person in my own right for once, with rights and needs as well as responsibilities."
(Miranda)

"You have to detach yourself from the situation. You can't change it. You have to put the focus on yourself. You can't be strong enough for two. Living with an alcoholic, you develop an incredible need to be in control all the time."
(Elsa, 25, shop manageress)

"Letting go is not a cold sort of turning away. I call it loving detachment. You can't solve everyone else's problems, that's all."
(Bridget, 39, information officer)

What is Detachment?

According to Al-Anon, detachment means letting go of an obsession with another's behaviour:

- Not to suffer because of the actions or reactions of other people
- Not to allow another person's recovery to be the excuse to be used or abused by them
- Not to do for others what they should do for themselves
- Not to manipulate situations so others will eat, go to bed, get up, pay bills, etc.
- Not to cover up for another's mistakes or misdeeds
- Not to create a crisis
- Not to prevent a crisis if it is in the natural course of events

Detachment is neither kind nor unkind. It is simply a means of coping with the adverse effects of alcoholism on your life. Detachment helps families look at their situation realistically and objectively, thereby

14

making intelligent decisions possible. In detaching, it is important not to feel that you are rejecting the alcoholic, it just allows your partner to be responsible for his own thoughts and actions. It is detachment with love.

D) ATTITUDES AND ATTITUDE CHANGE

Participation in group discussions with people in the same situation will help the family of a problem drinker examine their own attitudes. At home you no longer nag, lecture, boss, criticise or shout. You are looking at your life, not his. You are taking responsibility for your life. As the drinker's partner you no longer have to brace yourself for battle.

"The more I tried to do everything correctly the more I was blamed, so I tried harder to be a perfect wife, perfect mother. I believed everything reflected on me and I tried harder still. Thank God a kind person told me about Al-Anon group meetings where I could find love and support, where people understood me . . ."
(Pauline)

"One day I decided I wasn't going to do that any more. No one should get in the car with him when he's drunk. No one should get him up. No one should clean up the vomit. Walk away. Don't argue."
(Jenny)

E) CO-DEPENDENCY

"One of our women patients was told that it was her fault that her partner had hit her," says a co-dependency specialist. *"Of course it sounds ridiculous – it is ridiculous – but you would be amazed at the number of women who take that sort of accusation seriously."*

Here is a chance to assess your own situation:

- Do you feel guilty for his actions?
- Do you feel responsible for everything at home?
- Have you ever felt: If only I'd been there, things would have been different?
- Have you ever rung his workplace to make excuses because he was suffering from a drink or drug hangover?
- Does your life revolve around him?
- Does his life revolve around drink/drugs?
- Have you ever been told it was your fault that he hit you?
- Have you ever agreed?

Many people who live with problem drinkers and drug users find that they themselves have fallen into a self-destructive pattern of living which has come to be called "co-dependency". There is an organisation set up to help these people along the lines of Alcoholics Anonymous – Co-Dependents Anonymous

(CoDa). CoDa has identified two distinct ways of behaving which are ultimately unrewarding. These are undue *compliance* – pleasing others, and too much *control* – manipulating others. The following checklists of behaviours, characteristics and attitudes may help discover if there is co-dependency in your relationship. CoDa suggests the use of the words Always, Usually, Sometimes or Never against each statement to make the picture clearer.

Control Patterns

- I must be needed in order to have a relationship with others
- I value others' approval of my thinking, feelings and behaviour over my own
- I agree with others so they will like me
- I focus my attention on protecting others
- I believe most other people are incapable of taking care of themselves
- I keep score of "good deeds and favours", becoming very hurt when they are not repaid
- I am very skilled at guessing how other people are feeling
- I can anticipate others' needs and desires, meeting them before they are asked to be met
- I become resentful when others will not let me help them

- I am calm and efficient in others' crisis situations
- I feel good about myself only when I am helping others
- I freely offer others advice and directions without being asked
- I put aside my own interest and concerns in order to do what others want
- I ask for help and nurturing only when I am ill, and then reluctantly
- I cannot tolerate seeing others in pain
- I lavish gifts and favours on those I care about
- I use sex to gain approval and acceptance
- I attempt to convince others of how they "truly" think and "should" feel
- I perceive myself as completely unselfish and dedicated to the well-being of others

Score guide: If you tick 5 and under – you're pretty detached; 6–12 – you care a lot for others: be sure it doesn't take over your life – or theirs; 13–19 – you're in the danger zone.

Compliance

- I assume responsibility for others' feelings and behaviours
- I feel guilty about others' feelings and behaviours

Addiction – Drink

- I have difficulty in identifying what I am feeling/I have difficulty expressing feelings
- I am afraid of my anger, yet sometimes erupt in a rage
- I worry how others may respond to my feelings, opinions and behaviour
- I have difficulty making decisions
- I am afraid of being hurt and/or rejected by others
- I minimise, alter or deny how I truly feel
- I am very sensitive to how others are feeling and feel the same
- I am afraid to express differing opinions or feelings
- I value others' opinions or feelings more than my own
- I put other people's needs and desires before my own
- I am embarrassed to receive recognition and praise, or gifts
- I judge everything I think, say or do as "never good enough"
- I am a perfectionist
- I am extremely loyal, remaining in harmful situations too long
- I do not ask others to meet my needs or desires
- I do not perceive myself as a lovable and worthwhile person

- I compromise my own values and integrity to avoid rejection or others' anger

Score guide: 5 and under – you're a pretty robust character; 6–12 – take some time and thought to bolster your sense of self-worth: you matter too, you know! 13–19 – perhaps you need some skilled help to make you feel good about yourself?
(For further details write to the CoDa contact address/ring the CoDa telephone number given on page 171.)

CHILDREN AND DRINK PROBLEMS

How do you prevent your children from becoming problem-drinkers? Knowing that drinking is a family disease, you must make sure they are aware, at an appropriate age, that they are at risk. Talk about it, get it out in the open. Encourage them to attend a self-help group for the children of alcoholics when they are old enough. It might help to look at the family tree to see if drink problems have been a factor in the past.

"Both my parents are alcoholics, so there hasn't been a time when I haven't had to live with a drink problem. I spent so long denying there was anything wrong with me. I have to be needed – that is my

way of getting my sense of worth. For instance, last year I had a boyfriend who relied on me a good deal. I tend to end up with people I look after. There is drinking on both sides of my family. My mother's father had a drink problem, and my father's brother had a drink problem. I go to a group regularly – it's my way of keeping sane.
(Louise, 20, student)

"I'm at university at the moment. I'm a horrible high-achiever, a perfectionist . . . I tend to push myself harder because of my background (both my parents have a drink problem). Luckily, most of my friends are aware of the problem. It's very hard for me to strike a balance between caring for others and caring for myself. I tend to care for people rather than about them, if you see what I mean."
(Alison, 18, student)

"I used to feel responsible for making everything all right. I protect everyone. I was hideously responsible at a very young age – getting my brother and sister up and to school. We have all reacted in different ways to our parents' alcohol problem. My sister is anorexic. My brother has been in trouble a lot, but he will never discuss the drinking. The denial thing is very strong."
(Martha, 32, travel agent)

Some people also believe that other stress-related disorders are linked to alcohol abuse – however distantly – in the family tree:

"Bulimia, gambling, anorexia – they're all aspects of the same sickness. When dealing with children affected by these illnesses there's always alcoholism in the background. If people say 'no', there's denial as well."
(Anna, 38, teacher)

CASE HISTORY: Maureen
Maureen is 24 and an only child. She is a science graduate who works in telesales. When she was 21, her mother died in a road accident. Recently, her father, who was an alcoholic, died in hospital after falling and hitting his head at home when Maureen was out at work.

"After my father's death I was walking round in a state of complete shock. With hindsight, I believe I should have gone for some sort of counselling. At the time it was easy to think 'I'm in control, I can cope'. I felt guilty about Dad. He used to drink a lot when my mother was alive, but he could stop drinking completely if he wanted. What he couldn't do was drink lightly. Once he started to drink, he drank till he fell over. I think towards the end he began to think 'I've failed'. The only way to escape

22

was to drink. For as long as I can remember, he would fall face down in the salad at dinner parties. He wasn't an angry, depressive sort of drunk. He got a good feeling from drink, it relaxed him. I could see the drink killing him. At one point he was drinking three to five bottles of wine a day. I said 'Look, Dad, limit yourself to one bottle a day.' But he'd finish his one bottle by one o'clock. My father's brother wanted me to stay at home and 'keep an eye' on Dad – but I'd just got my first job. It was a terrible decision to have to face – but I stuck with the job. Right up to the end Dad didn't believe himself to be an alcoholic. He was very – well, almost naïve about it. I think he had a kind of mid-life crisis. He looked at what he'd achieved. He was 53, and he thought he had no way of bettering himself.

When he was in hospital, just before he died, I went through his papers and discovered that he hadn't paid the rent for three months, he had no money in the bank and he had been selling off family heirlooms. I wasn't aware that any of this had been going on. He would never discuss things like that with me. Even when he was dying he told me not to let his brother know he was in hospital. He was ashamed, I think.

The last three years have been very traumatic. When I have a family I want to be sure the same thing won't happen again. I hope I'll be a stronger

*character because of what has happened to me.
That's all."*

NIGHTMARE EXPERIENCES – LIVING WITH AN ALCOHOLIC

*"I do give way. When I'm feeling I can't cope I throw
in the towel. I'm not religious, but I do believe in the
power of prayer. I go down on my knees and say
'Please God, help me'."*
(Anna, 47, nurse)

*"The biggest challenge anyone can take on is living
with an alcoholic. When I was in the middle of it,
and feeling bad, everything was in a blur."*
(Sybil, 45, charity worker)

CASE HISTORY: Pauline
Pauline was brought up in a dysfunctional home,
although she did not realise it at the time. Both her
parents were from alcoholic homes, so love and
security in their childhoods were in very short
supply and they were unable to give any to her.
Pauline's story illustrates how you can slide into
coping for two – or more. The worst part of living
with an alcoholic is not necessarily the physical
dramas – the fights, the vomit, the urine-soaked
bedsheets – but the mental cruelty: the day-by-day

wearing down to exhaustion because you feel you have to take all the responsibility, the 'lost' hours or days when your partner disappears and then being blamed by him when things go wrong. One of Pauline's sons committed suicide in his early 20s after becoming an alcoholic.

"I married at the age of 20, for all the wrong reasons – I just wanted to be loved. After thirteen years and still feeling just as lonely, lost and unloved, I divorced and met a really kind charming man who vowed to love me and make me happy. I bought an apartment and moved in with my only son. The wonderful man I had met moved in along with his son. The boys thought it wonderful, they each had a brother at last. The boys shared a bedroom and became incredibly close.

This move gave me a great feeling of being really needed, everyone depended on me so much, I believed my dreams were at last fulfilled. I was suddenly wife, mother, stepmother, etc. My self-esteem began to increase.

However, I didn't know my partner was an alcoholic. I never really understood the problem. I was aware that his drinking spoilt my idealistic dream of family life and that his son was very emotionally disturbed, very insecure.

But before long this was the way we all felt. I believed it was my responsibility to 'hold the fort'. I would get up very early to feed and get our boys to school and to make sure my partner, who always worked nights, arrived home safely from work. Obviously a lot of money was being spent on drink so it was vital that I continued working full time. Despite the shortage of cash due to my partner's drinking we had to run two old cars because our schedules overlapped. My day began with phoning my partner's place of work, to check that he had actually left. I would then wake up the boys, make breakfast, do the school run and wait nervously until my partner returned home, usually the worse for wear, before driving myself to work. He was the sort of alcoholic who is actually drunk all the time – he just 'topped himself up' throughout the day and night. He would usually stop off somewhere on the way back from work to get a drink, maybe he sat in a layby with a can of export-strength lager. I tried to find out where he spent the time but I gave up asking because it just caused a row. He would visit the pub at 11.00a.m. and drink until 2.30p.m. before staggering home to bed. I spent most of the day phoning home, checking up on him etc. My husband said that it was vital that I woke him about 8.30p.m. for him to eat, wash and go to work. I would arrive home in the evening, cook, clean and begin to take on the impossible task of waking him up. This would sometimes take up to two hours. I would then feed him, order the boys to bed and *usually collapse in a heap by 11.00p.m. I had been on the go for seventeen hours. I started going to the doctor frequently – thinking that I needed a tonic and believing there was something wrong with me. To enable the boys to continue their education, and my partner to continue in his job, I tried to soldier on. However, I slowly went under. I was finally dismissed from my own job and my weight dropped to around 6½ stone.*

I looked exhausted and beaten. I then became self-employed and took all the work I could get, feeding the family on very little money. I was often attending the boys' schools over their absenteeism. I believe alcoholism is a family disease. I believe also that it creeps up on you quietly and gets louder and louder. Before long it was a series of rows, fights, abuse in the home. The more I tried to be a perfect wife, perfect mother the worse it became. I believed everything reflected on me and I tried harder still.

Thank God a kind person told me about Al-Anon, for family and friends of alcoholics. The group meetings where I could find love and support, where people understood me, as few others could, were a lifeline. I attended lots of meetings, became involved, slowly regained my confidence and a little more courage and began to learn to understand the illness my partner was suffering from. Gradually I was able to get my own life in some sort of order. The boys would occasionally come to a meeting but never chose to stay as I did. They would blot out the reality the best way they could.

After a couple of years in Al-Anon my partner finally reached rock bottom. He went to the Earls Court Boat Show one January. He rang me to say his car had been stolen and could I pick him up. He was tired, hungry, it was snowing and he was obviously drunk. I had to make a snap decision. I said 'I'm sorry, I'm busy, I can't come for you.' He slammed the phone down. A little while later he rang again. A little part of me said am I doing the right thing? but I still refused to go and rescue him. After a long and difficult journey, he got home and was very violent when he got in. He reported that the car had been stolen to the police. Each evening after that he wanted to borrow my car to get to work and I said 'No, you can't.' I kept hoping and praying I was doing the right thing. He would go on threatening and bullying me, and saying that if he didn't get to work he wouldn't get paid and the mortgage would get in arrears. After two weeks of practising this 'tough love' the phone rang. It was the police to say that his car had been found in the car park at Earls Court where he had left it. When he got in I told him to ring the police so he could find out for himself. He went and sat down with his head in his hands and said 'Am I going insane?' I said 'Yes, you are going insane.' For the next few days I referred all the neighbours to him when they noticed the car was back. I wasn't forcing any issue. I was just letting him take the consequences for his actions. He was feeling more and more stupid – he'd had a blackout, you see. He simply couldn't remember what he'd done with the car. He decided to go to a treatment centre three hours' drive away. They didn't allow him to contact even me for two weeks. Then he rang me and said 'It's so tough, and so painful. I'm going to have to give up and come home.' And I said 'You're going to have to face all that pain.' I wasn't going to allow him to dump all his feelings on me. He had pins and needles in his hands, lapses of memory and blackouts. He couldn't judge distances very well either. He was away for three months, during which time I was left to hold the fort again, however this time there was a lot of hope in my heart.

That was six years ago and he has been sober in AA ever since. We will never be the same again, but I find it helps me to share my experience, strength and hope with others, and to say, just for today I'm OK. I can get through today, I can try to erase the sad memories and pray to remember the good ones. My pain has lessened but I guess the scars will always be there."

THINGS COME TO A HEAD

Often an alcoholic becomes dangerous or threatens the family with physical violence. However, because of the tremendous strain they are under, it is sometimes the non-alcoholic partner who becomes violent towards their spouse or children.

In either case, the physical well-being of members of the family is threatened, and this often brings things to a head. Moving out or threatening to get a divorce may help a drinking partner appreciate the seriousness of the situation, but only if the threats are followed through.

"One New Year's Eve, we were both drunk. He fell asleep in an armchair with a lighted cigarette in his hand. Then he came up to bed, but the armchair must have already been smouldering. By the time the smell of smoke woke us, the whole living room was ablaze. The house nearly burned down with us all asleep inside. I realised that something had to be done or we were all going to end up dead. I gave him an ultimatum. Now we are both sober – and divorced."
(Mary, 38, teacher)

"I tried to kill my husband (he is an alcoholic) and then I failed so I tried to kill myself. I knew I couldn't

30

go on. I was screaming out for help but nobody understood."
(Jenny)

CASE HISTORY: Clare
Clare is an office manager aged 40. In her job she has responsibility for the staff and about 2,000 members of the public. She has been going to an ACCEPT group for family and friends of alcoholics for about four and a half years. She says:

"It has definitely helped me. I go once a week. Originally I went with the thought: I'm going to stop him drinking. Instead of that it has made me look at the reason why I was in the relationship at all and it's helped me look at myself. It's fulfilled its purpose in two ways.

We'd been together for fifteen years when I started to attend the group. My partner had always drunk a lot, but it changed from being just the occasional binge to being a serious problem.

My father drank, too – in the sense that if there was a bottle there he'd drink until he'd finished it. My mum criticised him all the time. I sympathised with Dad, because Mum used to nag him.

I think when I met my partner I thought I could help him but the situation became intolerable. He used to get violent until I told him I would get an injunction out if he touched me again. It wasn't like

31

you see on TV or anything. He'd just take the odd swipe in anger.

The original reason for my going to ACCEPT was because I tried to kill him on a couple of occasions. I was frightened. I tried to strangle him. I was being tormented. I always went to work, no matter what, you see. But he used to bang around the flat all night if he'd had a few, switching the television on and off, throwing himself on the bed. . . I got to such a point . . . It's a small flat, you see. You can hear every little noise. It was mental torture. But in the morning his neck was still bruised where I'd tried to strangle him. I think I went to ACCEPT because I saw their office on my way to work or something. I'd been to the doctor – had treatment for depression. The doctor gave me tablets and sent me for counselling. I was beginning to realise then that I had problems. My father was ill at the time. I hit rock bottom around then. I got no support from my partner. You deny it. You hide it. You think it's something you should keep to yourself.

He can only do temporary jobs now. He used to have a proper full-time job – well, several over the years, but he lost them all. He was sacked for having gone off on binges.

We do not have any children. Maybe I see him as a kind of child or a needy parent. I don't know. He goes on a binge about once every three to four weeks. He just drinks at home.

Addiction – Drink

He goes to Alcoholics Anonymous on and off. I don't know whether he's still having counselling. I am actually in the process of detaching myself from him. I can't tolerate it any more. I went away for six weeks at the end of last year by myself to the other side of the globe. I didn't have any ties, and no decisions to make. I presented myself as me, not as my mum's daughter or my brother's sister, or as the lady who runs the office at work. I used to feel fairly worthless, you see. Living with an alcoholic knocks your self-esteem. But on my own I was OK. That made me decide on separating, although of course I'd been thinking about doing it before. I'm going to buy his share of the flat. He's agreed to go – there's no problem about that.

I don't think that drink is going to kill him. Maybe it will. I don't understand why he has that first one. After that he can't seem to stop. But he always manages to come up OK afterwards. He's always managed to get work somewhere. He's not disabled by it in any way. He's had his liver checked, and there is no permanent damage apparently.

Now that I go to counselling I have a group of friends. Before, I didn't have any friends. I used just to go to work and then go home. That was my life. My friends are all people I've met through the group – we just try and support each other."

AFTER THE DRINKING STOPS

When looking to the future, you may be surprised and disappointed to discover that sobriety on its own is not the magic cure-all dreamed of in the worst days of drunken binges. Everyone involved needs the continued support of understanding friends. Patterns of unwanted behaviour and occasional depression are only to be expected. Emotional stress, the death of a parent, and worry at work, can bring old problems welling up to the surface. The partner of an alcoholic learns to spot a bad patch and seek help.

"Nowadays I don't try to cope. My worst days were before I joined Al-Anon. Now I go to one meeting a week, sometimes two. I draw my strength from them. I can share the load. I've gained more and more strength to cope with my difficulties through giving. We're in the group for our own personal growth."
(Esther, 41, secretary)

(Note from the author: When I started writing this chapter, I became quite ill and depressed. It wasn't until I sat down to read the Al-Anon literature that I realised that some of the problems in my family could stem from the fact that one of my grandfathers was an alcoholic. Realising this came as a tremendous relief. I felt that I had suddenly been given the key to understanding myself – and this was fourteen years after I had graduated in psychology! Moral: never, never underestimate the power of denial!)

2. DRUGS/SUBSTANCE ABUSE

DRUGS – DEFINITION OF

Drug or substance abuse often occurs in parallel with alcohol abuse. Problems caused by a partner's substance abuse are given an extra twist when the substances are illegal. Drugs such as tranquillisers, tobacco and caffeine (contained in tea and coffee) can pose health problems, but they are legal. Others such as cocaine, heroin, LSD and "Ecstasy" are not.

All drugs whether legal or illegal are mood enhancers, and work in various ways on the body's nervous system. Not all are physically addictive. Sometimes drugs such as tobacco, alcohol and cannabis are called "gateway" drugs, because they introduce the user to sensations which he may then seek to extend via stronger substances. There is also a wide range of physical and mental side-effects from taking drugs. Apathy, poor diet, self-neglect and poor housing are likely, in most cases, to add to the catalogue of user's woes.

Taking them group by group, the particular features of different drugs are:

OPIATES

These include heroin, morphine, methadone and pethidine. Although some people can lead successful lives while taking regular, even large doses of these drugs, for most a decline will occur. The sources of the drug will be illegal and probably expensive and the user may be willing to lie, steal and degrade himself and others to get hold of supplies.

The effects of opiates such as heroin are a sleepy euphoria accompanied by long-standing constipation. Tolerance of the drug develops rapidly so that severe addicts have to take up to twenty times their original dose to feel any effect. Added complications can arise if the drugs are taken intravenously: from unskilled and unhygienic injection, and include abscesses, septicaemia, hepatitis B and HIV/AIDS. The physical effects of coming off the drug include restlessness, wakefulness, running nose and eyes, diarrhoea, cramps and pains. Overdoses are the most common cause of death (one per cent of addicts a year, compared with an average "cure" rate of twenty per cent over five years). Sometimes death occurs if a user has been off the drug for a while and starts again at a high level of dose, when tolerance has faded. A strong mental and social dependence on the drug is sometimes harder to remedy than the physical need for the drug.

BARBITURATES

These include Tuinal, Seconal and Nembutal and are sometimes called "downers". They are taken to relieve tension and anxiety in much the same way as alcohol. They are available as prescription-only medicines. Their physical effects are similar to those of alcohol: drowsiness, stupor and sleep/ unconsciousness. Tolerance and dependence develops, and progressively larger doses have to be taken to achieve the original effect. Withdrawal ("hangover") effects include irritability, nervousness, sleeplessness, faintness, sickness, twitching and delirium. Because the cough reflex is suppressed, heavy users are prone to bronchitis and pneu-monia, hypothermia (because cold is not felt) and repeated accidental overdoses. These drugs are particularly lethal when mixed with alcohol.

AMPHETAMINES

These include "uppers" or "speed" such as Dexe-drine, Durophet, Ritalin Apisate and Tenuate. These drugs stimulate the nervous system, increase alertness, diminish fatigue, delay sleep and increase the ability to maintain vigilance or perform physical tasks over a long period, as well as elevating mood.

High doses cause nervousness, anxiety and temporary paranoid psychosis ("They're out to get me"). Withdrawal effects include hunger and fatigue. These drugs are available on prescription or illegally.

Cocaine – "coke", "snow" – is sometimes injected, but usually sniffed or smoked (in variations called "crack" or "freebase"). It produces a feeling of exhilaration and well-being, reduced hunger, indifference to pain and feelings of great physical strength and mental capacity. Large doses can give the user feelings of anxiety, agitation and persecution, and even hallucinations. After-effects include fatigue and depression. Cocaine is very expensive and this can lead to anti-social or criminal behaviour, to raise money to obtain the drug. Repeated sniffing can damage the nose membranes and the structure separating the nostrils.

CANNABIS

This is usually smoked as marijuana, sometimes called "weed" or "grass". It gives the effect of relaxation and euphoria. Widely believed by the medical profession to be as harmless (if not more so) than alcohol or nicotine, "it can be used in moderation by stable people with impunity" (Dr David Stafford-Clark). The health risks are on a par with those of smoking tobacco. In places where cannabis is used more than tobacco, such as

Jamaica, there is a high incidence of mouth and throat cancers. "Psychosocial" risks include those associated with its being illegal, and therefore part of the criminal sub-culture – dealers may try and interest smokers in other more harmful drugs. Use involves a certain amount of secrecy which may be cultivated for its own sake.

HALLUCINOGENS

Hallucinogens such as LSD or "acid" produce a "trip" effect that can last up to twelve hours. Reactions may include heightened self-awareness and mystical or ecstatic experiences. Unpleasant reactions may include depression, dizziness, disorientation and sometimes panic. The rare deaths that have occurred as a result of taking LSD are not from overdosing, but from people jumping from windows or in the case of Ecstasy (equally rare but it has happened), dehydration. "Magic mushrooms" belong to this category of drugs.

TRANQUILLISERS

Tranquillisers, "tranxs", and sleeping tablets are widely dispensed by harassed NHS doctors, particularly to women who report to surgeries feeling anxious and having difficulty sleeping. Brand names include Valium, Librium, Mogadon and Halcion. Side-effects include depression, moodiness and irritability, lethargy, digestive upsets, aches and pains, increased risk of accident, loss of concentration and memory lapses. Users risk addiction and may need medical help to "come off" after any prolonged use.

NITRATES

Amyl Nitrate, also known as "poppers", and Butyl Nitrate, "locker room", give a rushing sensation which heightens sexual pleasure. Excessive use can bring on severe vomiting, shock and unconsciousness, and has caused fatalities. Less severe side-effects include headaches and dermatitis. General worries reported by drug users' partners and families include stealing (to fund the habit), sexual infidelity while under the influence of the drug, drink (as a substitute for drugs) and death (as a possible effect of drug use).

"He started taking things, I began to notice money going from my bag and then the last straw was when he took my jewellery to sell. That's when I went to the police. I felt I had to draw the line."
(Sadie)

"I worried very much about how he was finding the money to pay for his habit. He must have been getting it from the business, and of course I lived in fear that he was stealing to pay for it."
(Emmy)

WHEN SOCIAL USE BECOMES ABUSE

Some people start smoking marijuana at university. It may seem a smart and harmless thing to do. Show-business and advertising people in particular often use cocaine with alcohol, to achieve a state of excitement and exhilaration and banish feelings of tiredness. So-called "designer drugs" such as Ecstasy are widely available at night-clubs. Problems arise when, due to the personality of the user or conditions of continued stress, or an interaction between the two, drugs are used in such a way as to cause physical or mental damage, and the user ceases to be able to function normally.

"He was taking acid twice a week and it was making him go crazy. I thought: now I know what it is like for someone to go mad."
(Marge)

"Peter was confident he could use cocaine for fun, to pep him up when he needed it at the end of a long day, and he maybe still had to take clients out. But gradually I could see that he needed it even to get through a normal day. It was costing him – us – a fortune."
(Emmy)

41

THE SIGNS OF ABUSE

There can be great tension between wanting to know the truth and wanting to trust your partner. It may be difficult to face up to the truth, anyway. In the same way, a drug user may do a lot to keep it from a partner, but part of them may at the same time want you to know about it. Tell-tale signs that a person is using drugs include:

- sudden unexplained weight loss
- secretive behaviour
- sudden but regular mood changes
- prolonged visits to the toilet with striking differences in "before" and "after" mood
- spending a lot of money
- new "undesirable" (i.e. drug-using) friends
- losing touch with friends who do not use drugs
- poor complexion
- neglecting appearance
- loss of interest in hobbies
- listless behaviour
- inability to stick at a job
- prolonged periods alone in bedroom
- absences from home

Sometimes drug users leave their paraphernalia lying about: roll-your-own cigarette papers or a little

42

pipe for smoking marijuana, or tin foil with traces of burning (for crack users), for example.

THE INITIAL SHOCK

Your partner's behaviour may have lead you to suspect that he is using drugs. When suspicion turns to certainty, strong emotions can be unleashed.

"I felt very angry and very frightened. I kept thinking: what happens if the police come to the house? We had two small children, and I was worried what would happen to them if we were disgraced with a court case."
(Anna)

"The worst thing was the suspense every day. Would he come home on time? Would he be very late? Would he come home at all? And how much would he have spent if he'd been on a spree?"
(Madeleine)

"He had one particular 'friend' (I didn't like him at all) and I just knew that if he came to the house they would shut themselves away listening to records and getting high. Simple as that."
(Cathy)

"It was only when I found out the truth about Bill, that it finally came to the crunch. I was strong, and I said, 'You're not going to lie to me this time. Tell me the truth'. And I think that frightened him. I think when you know the truth it makes you all the more determined to do something."
(Coping with a Nightmare – Family Feelings about Long-Term Drug Use)

"You're so upset it's happening, you don't want to believe it. And because addicts are so convincing in the end you go along with it. In your heart of hearts you know that they're lying, and it's that burden of are they telling the truth or aren't they? Do I believe them or don't I? And it's a total torturing nightmare that you live, day in and day out."
(Coping with a Nightmare)

Sometimes a partner may consider going to the police if they think they know who is supplying the drugs. Experiences and opinions vary as to the advisability of "grassing" on your partner. Sometimes the wish to bring everything out into the open and involve the courts can be overwhelming. Remember, though, that most users also deal, in however small a way, to pay for their habit. There is also the risk that going to the police could be seen as a betrayal of trust and a rejection. Experts at the Blenheim Project, a West London-based drugs information and counselling service say:

"We have not found going to the police a helpful approach in solving individual drug problems. If a person is convicted for a drug offence (possession or dealing), the options open to the courts are those applicable to criminals, e.g. fines and prison. The law is not designed to help people with drug-related problems. If someone has a drug problem, we believe it is better for them to seek help directly, rather than go through the uncertainty and trauma of a court appearance and possible imprisonment."

It should be remembered that the underlying causes of a partner's drug use are not likely to be addressed in prison. A jail sentence and criminal record may make things worse. In any case, drugs are available in many prisons (illegally, of course).

DEPENDENT/ADDICTIVE PERSONALITIES

As with alcohol, doctors sometimes find it useful to describe certain drug users as "dependent" or "addictive" personalities. Someone who has a dependent personality looks for the solution to his problems outside himself. Someone who has an addictive personality tends not to be able to use stimulation of any kind – food, gambling, drugs or drink – in moderation.

Many drug users appear to choose drugs to relieve turbulent feelings against a background of family disturbance. Normal human values are dispensed with. Jobs are given up, in favour of resting and criticising the 'bourgeois system', sex is taken in a world of shifting uncommitted relationships, and others' money, property and interests are subordinated to theirs. A certain characteristic intense selfishness and self-preoccupation often exist alongside the drug-taker's declared belief, that other people and external circumstances are wholly to blame for his behaviour. These same "guilty parties" are also – paradoxically – the ones the drug user turns to for help. Rescue attempts by various well-meaning friends, lovers, and parents are doomed to fail, unless they all accept that *their* behaviour as well as the addicts, holds the key to recovery, because they may be 'co-depending'.

When the drug-taker becomes addicted, his preoccupation with obtaining drugs starts to override all other aspects of daily life. *"Drugs are always easy to start but hard to give up"* (Dr David Stafford-Clark).

CASE HISTORY: Petronella and Max
Petronella's husband Max is a stockbroker. They are both in their early 40s. She says:

"I always knew that stockbroking put a strain on Max's nerves. It's the sort of job where you have to put on an act the whole time to jolly the clients along. During the 1980s we had a fabulous life style in some ways. Looking back on it, of course, it was very superficial. But for us at the time it was a kind of fairy tale. The sky was the limit. People did silly things, they had so much money. Going to Paris for lunch, that sort of thing. Then came the crash in 1987. It was obviously a shock for all sorts of reasons – people's portfolios were wiped out by as much as a third of their previous value. Max was working even longer hours. He got very thin and became extremely depressed and moody. I knew money was going to be tight with us as with everyone else, but I was really surprised at how little we had. Eventually he broke down and told me that he had been spending a lot of money on cocaine. Our bank account was more overdrawn than I'd realised and he had somehow managed to borrow more money by using our house as collateral. I threatened to leave him unless he checked himself into a clinic, which he did. My parents paid for the treatment. The thing about cocaine is that it makes you feel really good even when you're not, if you

see what I mean. Max had started dabbling in the days when he had so much money he didn't know what to spend it on. Everyone else in his office was doing it and I suppose there was an element of peer group pressure – being one of the lads. There is great pressure to look good and sound good in the financial services business. You must always be bright and cheerful and on top of things. Cocaine isn't really a social drug: you just go off and sniff it up in the loo. But it is insidious. You start by using it for fun, then you find you need it. Max has had to keep his problems absolutely secret from the firm. They knew he was having some sort of treatment. Our doctor, bless him, said it was 'mental exhaustion'! The clinic he attended has told us that he could have to go through as many as seven courses of treatment before he gets rid of the habit. Residential treatment lasts for two or three weeks. Then there is a group (Cocaine Anonymous) and you come back whenever you have fallen back into the habit, or for consultation with a counsellor. The worst part of coming off are 'cocaine dreams'. He wakes up thinking he is about to use it and of course there is a terrible let-down. Cocaine gets its hooks into you really fast. The 'high' is very high and very short. People spend thousands of pounds – they sell their house and steal things. There are health risks. Max was getting pains in his chest, and there is one poor girl of 25 who he met in the clinic who has had a stroke. She'll be in a home for the rest of her life. Max takes anti-depressants now. The worst thing is that he knows he will never have that feeling of confidence again. 'I could do anything – nothing could touch me' was the way he described it."

GETTING PROFESSIONAL HELP

Once the problem is faced up to, quite a few things can be done.

Adfam is the national organisation for the families and friends of drug users. Legal advice and information can be obtained from Release. Another port of call if you are worried that your partner is using drugs is a helpline. The names of some national helplines are given at the end of this book. Others are available in public libraries and the front of telephone books. Getting reliable information that you can think about quietly at home is a great relief. No one solution is right for everyone. You may prefer to start your own self-help group with like-minded people.

Beware of some offers of help: one worried partner was given a handout on the street naming a drug rehabilitation centre which she later discovered was run by the Scientology movement – possibly jumping out of the frying pan into the fire!

Doctors can be very helpful, if only because they

are able to apply a trained and dispassionate mind to the problem. What you want to hear and what you do hear may be two very different things, though.

"I thought our GP would immediately reach for his telephone and book Charlie into a clinic and that would be the answer. Of course I realise now how hopelessly unrealistic that was. I know now that it is going to be a very long haul, and it will be up to Charlie to solve his problems. But one can't help hoping that there is an instant solution to things, can one?"
(Marge)

Taking drugs is a problem of the attitude of both the abuser and his partner, as well as physical dependence, so counselling and therapy may be involved for both partners.

RECOVERY

Professionals warn that a drug user whose habit is ruining his own life and his partner's, may only *appear* to respond to an ultimatum. He may go through the motions of compliance with medical advice only to default on attendance, or discharge himself from a hospital or clinic, after a spell of manipulative attempts to obtain the drug or substitutes for it. Patric Hemsworth is the programme co-ordinator at the Charter Clinic in Chelsea:

"Recovery rates vary enormously between types of drug and the individuals concerned. Of course, it helps if the individual really wants to get better himself. But even if it is the family who actually arrange and pay for the treatment, at least then the user can be in an atmosphere where he can sit quietly and consider his position. Once users recognise the mess they are in and break through their denial – that is, when they accept they have a problem – their motivation changes. A user's life is out of control – that's why we involve the family, because we nearly always find that they have fallen into the trap of supporting the patient in his drug use. (See "Co-dependency" section on page 16.)

"We always say to people: 'recovery is for the family'. We say to the user's partner: what are you going to do if he starts on drugs again? Make plans! We plan, plan, plan. Their lives have been out of control. Some partners when I ask them that say: I'm going to leave. So I come back with: how are you physically going to do it? Will you go or will your partner? I've had women say: I'll go and I won't let you know where I've gone – and meant it. But they have to mean it.

Some of the women who come to the clinic with their partners have taken total control: they pay all the bills, make the excuses and check everything out. In a drug-using family it gets to the point where the children learn to change their behaviour when the drug-using parent comes home.

We teach self-awareness and self-esteem. The watchword is 'You deserve better than this'. Addiction erodes self-esteem. Patients begin to make progress when they begin to like themselves again. A lot of people check in for treatment because they are depressed. Drugs and depression often go together. When people have come off their drug, be it cocaine or alcohol or both, we can look at what made them feel it necessary to start using it in the first place. We look at their addiction and their life problems together."

DUAL DIAGNOSIS

"Sometimes we find that people with a drug problem are suffering from quite severe mental illness – it is the illness which has brought about the drug use rather than the other way about. We call this process of separating out the strands 'dual diagnosis'. Dual diagnosis has only been recognised in the last four or five years as an essential part of addiction treatment. What it boils down to, basically, is

that a lot of people who are mentally ill *use alcohol and drugs as a kind of self-medication."*

DRUGS AND DRINK TOGETHER

Every other chemical "queues" for alcohol. This means that the body always metabolises the alcohol first. So, anyone who drinks when they are taking prescribed medication risks playing havoc with the treatment, because their medication will be building up in their system in quantities the doctor cannot have foreseen. It will also mean that the medication will have no effect until the alcohol has been processed.

DRUG-RELATED EMOTIONAL HANG-UPS

Partners of drug users experience difficult times. Broken promises give rise to feelings of betrayal. The drug user appears to be ruining, or at the very least, risking, his health and career. The uncertainty of the life you lead together often causes frustration and anger.

Treatment involves looking at anger either through individual therapy, group therapy or a combination of the two. Many people find it helps to go on having regular therapy sessions for years, particularly if they were physically or emotionally abused as children, in which case the anger is likely to have been suppressed for many years. Therapists categorise anger as a feeling – passive anger, aggressive anger and cold anger (which can be called resentment).

People can only have healthy relationships if they learn how to deal with anger, and to address why someone is making them angry. In our culture we learn to bottle up anger. People have to learn that it is OK to express it in the same way that it is OK to express being happy or sad. That means being able to express appropriately, in ways that are not detrimental to oneself or to others.

HANDING BACK CONTROL

If your partner is an addict he must be allowed to regain control over his own life. You may find it difficult to let go but it is important to his self-esteem. Sometimes, women who marry addicts often divorce one and then go off and marry another. This is because caring for an addict is fulfilling a need within themselves, to be useful.

The words "tough love" are easy to say, maybe less easy to apply, but those who have put the concept into practice say they get the hang of it gradually. Basically, it means pausing to think before you comply with a request – overt or implied – from your partner, which allows him to pass responsibility for his actions back on to you. You may find it useful to read the section on "Tough Love" and "Detachment" in the previous chapter. Loving detachment means everything from leaving his own vomit for him to clear up, to insisting that he himself rings in sick if he is unfit for work through drug use. You may have become what the professionals call "co-dependent". This means feeling responsible for another adult's life.

FAMILY ROLE-PLAY

There are many addicts who have not dealt with the effects of a damaged childhood. Everyone in an addict's life takes on a role. Patric Hemsworth says:

"I have had 12-year-old kids sitting in my consulting room behaving like parents while their natural/biological father sits there acting like a kid. I had one threesome in here the other day. The son sat beside his mother on the sofa between her and his father, who sat on a separate chair. They had arranged themselves the way they were living: at

home, the little boy was trying to protect his mother and also trying to control his father's drinking and drug-taking. The son was 'parenting' his parents. These are long-standing habits. An awful lot of people who have addiction problems now, have been brought up in homes where one or other parent was themselves an alcoholic or drug addict. People come here for treatment aged 40 who have been drinking or using drugs heavily since they were 15. Behaviour that long-standing has to be given up over a long period of time. Everything starts to get easier once the whole family realise what a new life would be like. The help they need varies between individuals."

Some people actually get addicted to going to group therapy. The watchword here is balance – learning to balance work and family and self.

FAMILIES, DRUGS AND THE LAW

Technically, the law states that "possession", giving away or selling a drug covered by the Misuse of Drugs Act, is against the law. If you know that someone in your house is using, supplying or sharing such a drug on your "premises", and you do not inform the police, you are committing an offence. If you find drugs they should either be handed to the police or destroyed.

The Misuse of Drugs Act gives police the power to stop people who they have reason to suspect may be carrying drugs. Class A drugs such as LSD and cocaine carry the highest penalties. Class B drugs include cannabis and barbiturates, unless they have been prepared for injection in which case they are classified as Class A. Other minor drugs such as mild tranquillisers or stimulants are Class C. Penalties vary from seven years in jail and an unlimited fine for possession of Class A drugs, to a three-month sentence and a fine of £50 or so for possessing the least dangerous drugs.

The Medicines Act restricts the supply of certain powerful drugs to "prescription only" by doctors and registered pharmacists.

WHEN YOUR CHILD IS A DRUG USER

Different members of the family may react in different ways to a drug problem. Very often it does seem to be the mother who feels most affected by the knowledge that one of her children is using drugs, and gets most involved in trying to make things better.

"I think some men find it difficult to handle the situation. They are not so emotionally involved. Sometimes their reaction is to behave as though it was nothing to do with them."
(Jane)

"He nearly went mad when he knew she had started having sex. So I knew he would go spare if he found out she was doing drugs."
(Diana)

EXAMINING ATTITUDES TO DRUG USE

Much of what is said in the chapter on drink applies equally to drugs. Don't forget that you and other members of the family have rights too. There is sometimes a need to reassert those rights. Many support groups recognise this need as paramount over the issues posed by the problem drug user. For instance, how can a partner or a family limit the damage that a drug user causes? Alongside this, there is also a need for self-control as well. A person may inadvertently have been facilitating a partner's drug use. Withdrawal of support – "detaching with love" – could change that. Family and friends support groups often discuss the concept of "enabling". This concerns the role played in a drug user's life by well-meaning people who actually help him to continue his drug habit. Groups can reduce the sense of isolation and helplessness felt by a drug user's partner. Everyone needs to laugh or cry occasionally about the things that happen. Getting together gives you muscle to fight for the issues you feel need publicising. Skilled help is available for setting up a group for families and friends of drug users. Most local Councils for Voluntary Services (CVS) or Rural Community Councils (RCC) can help put together a constitution and advise on the advantages and disadvantages of becoming a charity. Or the National Council of Voluntary Organisations (NCVO) in London offers skilled help in setting up a group. (See end for details.)

MENTAL DISTRESS

Part Two

MENTAL DISTRESS

1. REACTIVE AND PSYCHOTIC DISORDERS

"Stress", "depression", "nervous breakdown": these are familiar ways of describing the mental state of a person who finds himself unable to carry on life as usual. If your partner suffers from a mental disorder it can cause confusion and can dislocate even the most stable relationship.

There are many events which can lead to temporary (or 'reactive') mental distress, ranging from unemployment or worries at work to bereavement. One too many loads to bear may tip even the most stable person over into breakdown or attempted suicide. Matters may be made more difficult if your partner's illness has impaired his judgement, and he is unaware that he needs treatment.

However, there are mental conditions which don't have any obvious external cause, and seem to be due more to the internal imbalance of the body (brain) chemicals. This group includes "endogenous" depression, schizophrenia and Alzheimer's disease. (Partners of Alzheimer's sufferers have special difficulties, and the second half of this part is devoted to them.)

Because of the nature of your partner's illness you will have to contend with many difficulties, including stigma and misunderstanding of your partner's condition, reduction in your standard of living if either one of you is unable to keep a job, and social isolation caused by the prejudice and ignorance of your friends and neighbours. Mental illness affects the brilliant achievers as much, if not more, than the average person. Winston Churchill suffered from disabling periods of dejection which he called his "black dog", an expression coined two hundred years earlier by another sufferer, the famous literary personality Dr "Dictionary" Johnson.

"When John is in one of his depressions, from which he has suffered all his life, he could be mistaken for a tramp. He can hardly communicate, he neglects his appearance – he does not shave – and he even finds it difficult to stay standing up for long – he can slip to the ground and just sit there."
(Faith, wife of a senior lawyer)

DIFFERENT REACTIVE DISORDERS

States of mental distress such as "reactive" depression and obsessions happen in response to an identifiable stressful external cause sometimes with catastrophic suddenness, as if a sufferer has been holding back anxieties and feelings for so long, that when they are allowed through they overwhelm him.

DEPRESSION
This affects mood and response to stimulation. It is accompanied by a loss of appetite for sex or food. Everything seems to be an effort and nothing seems worthwhile. Sufferers complain they cannot think straight, and that they feel sad or despairing. In extreme cases, a person may think of – or attempt – suicide.

"Bill retired from the army and got a job as the business manager of a London law firm. He was always a perfectionist, liable to worry about getting every small detail right. About a year ago he started to go to work earlier and earlier and got back later and later. He complained about every little noise in the house; I wasn't allowed the radio on because he said music disturbed him. He spent what little time he had at home on his own. Then he came home in

the middle of the day and burst into tears. He had been called in to the senior partner because things had got behind and muddled at the office. He looked dreadful – he had done for days – and said that he felt that life was not worth living. He said he felt exhausted and that the job had got completely on top of him. I rang our doctor who got him over for a chat, and diagnosed severe depression. He advised him to rest for a week quietly and gave him some medication. He had an appointment with a consultant psychiatrist who suggested we both went to a psychotherapist for a while, to talk through the things that were worrying Bill. He is much better, but he keeps an eye on himself now. He knows he can get into a downward spiral if he gets overloaded."
(Mary, school secretary, 51)

OBSESSIVE-COMPULSIVE DISORDER

This is another common "reactive" disorder. It entails endless checking and re-checking by the sufferer, of small details, to the extent that the checking begins to interfere with his everyday life and is usually triggered off by a trauma, which, however, usually bears no relation to the obsession. In an extreme case, it took someone two and a half hours to shave:

". . . much of this time being taken up in checking the exact setting of the razor, in making sure that all the adjustable parts were screwed to a particular degree

of perfect balance and tension. Similarly when punching a card either to clock in or to clock out at work, the card had to be taken back six or a dozen times to make sure that it had been properly punched, and that the time and date upon it corresponded accurately with the actual hour and day on which the operation had been undertaken."
(Dr David Stafford-Clark)

Other ritual activities that have been recorded include turning taps on and off repeatedly to be absolutely sure they are off; checking and re-checking that the soles of the shoes are clean of feared dog dirt; sealing and re-sealing letters; washing out a bath repeatedly with disinfectant before use. Your partner may know that his fears are irrational but feels a compulsion to continue. Current medical advice is that you should keep the performance of rituals under review and control, not to turn a blind eye to them or behave as though everything is normal. In the early stages, careful and supportive discussion of the behaviour every time it happens does help your partner to eliminate the rituals. For longer-standing habits, treatment can include anxiety-reducing drugs and behaviour therapy in the form of a desensitization or "flooding", whereby your partner is gradually exposed to the thing he fears but prevented from engaging in the ritual, thereby putting the fear into perspective.

STRESS

Stress and all the psychosomatic illnesses which go with it are the cause of the most widespread forms of reactive mental distress. If your partner is under stress he will feel inadequate and sometimes totally overwhelmed. Suddenly, one day, he has woken up and felt that he simply cannot cope any longer. One senior businessman at the peak of his career locked himself in the bathroom one day and would not come out. Other people may go to their doctor complaining of migraine or back pain and the doctor diagnoses stress as the underlying cause of their physical aches and pains.

Patric Hemsworth of the Chelsea Charter Clinic says:

"The sort of person who suffers from stress-related disorders is a perfectionist. This kind of person can do things quite adequately but feels a need to do them even better. Typically, he may be a business-man who drives himself and his family mad because nothing is ever good enough. He tells his wife she is inadequate and his staff that they are inadequate. We see people in our clinic who have ended up

doing virtually everything themselves, because they have decided that no one does anything well enough. Such a person cannot delegate responsibility in even quite trivial matters, things get worse and worse, they see less and less of their family and they comfort themselves with drink and drugs to spur them on. Sometimes such a person gets obsessional – they have to check and re-check everything so often that nothing ends up getting done. The advantage of treating this kind of a person in a residential setting is that it forces them to take 'time out'. They can begin to recognise what is happening to them. We get a lot of people who think that if they let go, they will lose control. Maybe in the back of their mind there is a fear that the person they delegate to will do their job better. They have to begin to learn: do I feel happy enough with me to let go?"

Apart from headaches and back-aches, other typical stress-related physical disorders include poor sleeping – waking three or four times during the night and tossing and turning, nausea and stomach-aches and general minor health problems. Patric Hemsworth says:

"People use valium, thinking that their problem is not getting enough sleep, instead of looking at the reasons behind their sleep problem. It could be a

workaholic that needs to be at work. We see people who tell us that they dread weekends. One father we had in here used to spend his whole weekend sitting in front of this home computer, instead of with his family."

Your partner needs to recognise what his own problem is, and to accept that there are some things he can't do anything about. One man reported that he was angry for a week at his wife, because he was late for an important appointment one Monday morning. The shirt he wanted to wear had fallen off the hanger in the wardrobe and his wife had to re-iron it, thus making him late. Could he not have worn another shirt or ironed it himself?

"We teach people to deal with a situation like that and then let it go. It wasn't anyone's fault – it wasn't a big deal. Carrying anger around for days about such a trivial event is far more damaging than the event itself."

PREVENTING STRESS

Never forget that you, yourself, as the partner having to take the strain in your relationship, will be prone to stress. This section could be relevant to both you and your partner. Remember, prevention is better than cure, so read and apply accordingly.

a) People who live their life saying I should have done this, or I should have done that, must learn that making mistakes in life is not a capital offence. Everyone makes mistakes – that is the only way you learn to do things right.

b) Blaming everyone else for things that go wrong is pointless. *"The first thing is to get people who are like that to recognise that they have a problem,"* says Patric Hemsworth. *"But it can be hard when they are starting to accept that it may be them who have the problem, when they are already 60 years of age! They have to learn new behaviour."*

c) One way of starting the re-learning process is to ask: are you happy with work? How do you deal with other people? Do you *like* other people? Maybe you don't like your partner, but feel you should stick by him. Do you like yourself? If not, you're not going to like many other people.

Feelings are another vital area, especially for the buttoned-up British. Families attending stress therapy classes together are asked: how do you communicate with each other?

d) Communicate. Some family therapists carry out an exercise whereby everyone has the chance to talk for five minutes and – more importantly – everyone else in the family has to listen. Men on the whole are not good listeners. Recent research has shown that many are chronic interrupters, especially of the women in their family. But an exercise in talking and listening is only part of the story. People often need to learn how to verbalise their feelings. Many men have never actually said that they are happy and proud to be a husband and a father to their wife and family. *"We say to men: so how did you expect them to know?"* says Patric.

Communication is vital – especially of how you feel. *"We get people to role play. For instance, we will ask them to remember the last thing that made them angry and get them to verbalise their anger – put it into words."* Many men find it uncomfortable to say when they are feeling sad. Bottling up feelings for men or women leads to the headaches, back-aches and other symptoms that busy doctors treat with palliatives, instead of probing root causes. One doctor nicknames cystitis "pissed off disease", because it often goes with a feeling of discontent.

"The essential skill that people need to avoid stress is to learn to recognise feelings and then communicate them."

COUNT YOUR STRESS

Psychologists have worked out a scoring system for events likely to produce stress. Any change, even pleasurable and sought-after change, puts a strain on your system. Adapting to new data means "work" for your mind and your emotions. If two or more of these life events come along in quick succession, your "stress count" will rise to danger levels and you will need to make a determined and conscious effort to ease off. Don't ask yourself to cope with more than is reasonable.

LIFE EVENT	STRESS VALUE (scale 1–100)
Death of spouse	100
Divorce	73
Marital separation	65
Prison term	63
Death of close family member	63
Personal injury or illness	53
Marriage	50
Fired at work	47
Marital reconciliation	45
Retirement	45
Change in health of family member	44
Pregnancy	40
Sex difficulties	39
Gain of new family member	39
Business readjustment	39
Change in financial state	38
Death of close friend	37
Change to different line of work	36
Change in number of arguments with spouse	35

Mortgage over £20,000	31
Foreclosure of mortgage or loan	30
Change in responsibilities at work	29
Son or daughter leaving home	29
Trouble with in-laws	29
Outstanding personal achievement	28
Wife/partner begins or stops work	26
Begin or end school	26
Change in living conditions	25
Revision of personal habits	24
Trouble with boss	23
Change in work hours or conditions	20
Change in residence	20
Change in schools	20
Change in recreation	19
Change in church activities	19
Change in social activities	18
Mortgage or loan less than £20,000	17
Change in sleeping habits	16
Change in number of family get-togethers	15
Change in eating habits	15
Holiday	13
Christmas	12
Minor violations of the law	11

(Adapted from Holmes & Rahe, *Journal of Psychosomatic Research*, Vol 11, Pergamon Press, 1967.)

SOME SIGNS AND SYMPTOMS OF STRESS

Physical
Migraines or headaches
Tummy upsets,
    constipation,
    diarrhoea
Insomnia
Overtiredness,
    exhaustion, fatigue,
    lethargy
Loss of appetite
Skin complaints
General aches and pains
Hyperventilation,
    shortness of breath
High blood pressure
Excessive consumption
    (alcohol, nicotine,
    food)
Tremor, twitching,
    palpitations
(From *Coping with*
    Stress by Dave MacDonald, ISDD, 1992.)

Mental & Emotional
Inability to concentrate
Compulsive worry or
    anxiety
Easily moved to tears
Marked depression
Sudden mood swings
Paranoid thoughts
Victim mentality
Unprovoked outbursts
    of anger
Avoiding commitments
Difficulties with
    decision-making
Feeling of failure
Loss of sense of humour

COPING WITH STRESS

Coping strategies will vary from person to person, but they should include both physical and mental/emotional aspects.

- Deep relaxation – this could be swimming (the activity so highly rated for relieving stress that some NHS doctors actually prescribe it by using pool vouchers), playing sport with others or going for a walk with the dog – anything that gives profound physical relief from stress
- Release self-damaging emotions, especially as soon as possible after a stressful situation has thrown a person into turmoil
- Develop supportive relationships through which advice, emotional release and a nice feeling of belonging can be obtained
- Be assertive in your own interests without getting aggressive
- Live within your means – i.e. adjust your lifestyle if possible to give you spare cash for occasional treats, such as meals out, cinema visits, holidays, *Hello!* magazine, etc.
- Do not work, work, work. Have time off – lead a balanced life
- Put events and emotions into perspective

There is extensive literature on stress management as well as courses to help you deal with stress. Finding out what might suit you will be the first stress-reducing step.

Counselling can help a person remember an event or a relationship from the past which may still be causing stress in the present. Hemsworth says:

"Many more men have been sexually abused than people imagine. Sexual abuse varies from interference as a child by close relatives, to male rape after parties. Sometimes consensual homosexual acts occur when people have had too much to drink. Memories of what seems shameful behaviour may cause a partner to be anxious and guilty in later heterosexual relationships."

Case 1: "A" hated his body. His parents were both alcoholics. As a child he would find his parents – one or both – naked in the family bathroom vomiting into the toilet. He had a real problem with sex because of this association in his mind between nakedness and (literally) nauseating behaviour.

Case 2: "B" received in-patient treatment for cocaine addiction, which appeared successful. He re-presented to the clinic having transferred his addictive behaviour from cocaine to sex! He was spending up to four hours a day waiting to watch a woman undress by a window. His time was further disrupted during the working day by obsessive thoughts about watching her get undressed.

CASE HISTORY OF HYSTERIA:
Hysterical reactions are sometimes the result of a frightening experience or an accident:

"Bob was working on a construction site – he is an engineer – and he had a very frightening experience with a hoist, getting his arm trapped. It was stopped just in time to prevent him being severely injured, but his fingers were stiff and his neck ached on one side where he had been pulled. Although the hospital could not find any serious injury, he found he could not move his right arm. This went on for seven years while the firm disputed liability. The doctors were recommending he had his arm amputated and re-admitted him to hospital. Then the firm finally agreed to pay him a lump sum unconditionally, and he seemed to relax for the first time since the accident. Because he showed signs of getting the use of his arm back, the operation was called off and he gradually got the feeling back into his arm, and now, three or four months later, he can use it again."
(Pat, 37, catering manager)

A specialist comments: *"Often, hysterical symptoms provoke contempt and hostility, but always they are a warning that a human being is in distress."* In cases of "reactive" mental distress, the only real cure is the relief of, or coming to terms with, the underlying stress. However, superficial treatment – from hypnosis to physiotherapy – may be effective in relieving the stress.

Psychotic Illnesses

Some forms of mental illness show themselves early in life. Chronic depression and schizophrenia can start in the teens or early twenties.

Chronic or "endogenous" depression is widely suspected of having a chemical basis. One common form, manic depression, can alternate depression with episodes of feverish activity falling over into mania. This condition is different from the normal fluctuations of mood experienced by everyone. Once recognised, manic depression can be controlled by drugs to even out the peaks and troughs experienced by the sufferer. During manic episodes the sufferer may spend unrealistic amounts of money on a flamboyant life style, and adopt totally unrealistic attitudes towards his life, as the following case history relates.

CASE HISTORY:
"A young surgeon aged 34 in a university town in the Midlands began to arrange his operating list earlier and earlier in the mornings, and to instruct the sister in

charge of the Out-Patient Department to book more and more cases for him at his Out-Patient Clinic. By the time he was arriving at the operating theatre and expecting to start operating at 5.30a.m., and had informed the Out-Patient Department that no less than twenty-five cases were to be booked for his afternoon clinics, it became evident that his general judgement was no longer to be trusted. He proved to be sleeping less than three hours a night, to be drinking and spending to excess in his leisure periods. By the time of his referral for professional advice, which he insisted was quite unnecessary, he had begun to delegate both operating sessions and his Out–Patient Clinic to junior colleagues, in order to devote more time to studying investments on the stock exchange, and the probable form of horses in the local races, hoping to raise vast sums of money to improve the general surgical equipment and facilities of the hospital. On examination he was excitable, restless, distractible, and at once arrogantly confident, insistently flippant, and readily exasperated. He had to be admitted to the psychiatric department of an appropriate hospital, where he was with some difficulty persuaded to remain and receive treatment. At the time of his admission, his professional work was in chaos and his personal debts exceeded £10,000." (Dr David Stafford-Clark)

SCHIZOPHRENIA

This is a major psychotic illness meaning that a sufferer (possibly your partner) loses touch with reality and no longer realises he is ill. Because of its early onset few sufferers manage to start a family of their own, but if you already have, your partner will involve you in his own distress. The condition can be greatly improved with drugs, but your partner can drift away from you, the carer. There is an increased interest in carers' rights in illnesses such as schizophrenia. Families and partners can feel frustrated at being kept at arm's length by the conventions of medical etiquette, and at the failure of the law to provide a safety net for their loved ones. Moves are afoot to enable an order to be made to protect the schizophrenic from drifting away from treatment and care, and prevent further tragedies such as the recent case of a sufferer whose legs had to be amputated, after he was found sleeping "rough" in the coldest winter weather. Many young people sleeping rough are sufferers.

IMMATURE PERSONALITY

Criminal psychopaths, the sort of people who commit serial murders, are fortunately few and far between – but what professionals call "immature personalities" are met with often enough. These are people who want what they want immediately, whatever the consequences. They seem unable to postpone gratification for the sake of future stability or success. They are unable to sustain social relationships. They tend to reject medical or psychological help except as an emergency measure in an extreme crisis. Even then they will exploit such help rather than co-operate with it if they can. They appear to have strong inner demands – they act on impulse and very rarely display foresight or wisdom. They attempt instead to distort and misinterpret reality to make it fit their own self-centred concepts.

If this description is depressingly apt for an adolescent not a million miles from home, do not worry – adolescents grow up. This kind of description is only worrying if it fits someone who ought to know better – someone who has reached their 20s or 30s, and possibly has family responsibilities. A chronically immature partner needs professional help.

CARERS

Some sorts of mental distress need more or less constant sympathetic caring. If your partner is suffering from endogenous depression he can experience recurring difficulties throughout his lifetime. So-called "acute" episodes of mental illness call for emergency measures, and may call for your full-time support while the emergency lasts. However, in extreme cases, a stay in hospital is often recommended.

Jacqueline Atkinson, a specialist in this area, believes that the *"responsibility the health service owes to relatives who care for mentally ill patients is gradually being acknowledged"*. The areas under liveliest discussion include:

- Access of medical information to relatives – is the aim of the medical service to be seen in terms of carers' interests as well as patients'? What if the sufferer seems unwilling to let his partner have access to medical information?
- Autonomy – when does a patient cease to be capable of exercising his own judgement about himself and his treatment? When should "confidentiality" be extended to include a partner?

CARE IN THE COMMUNITY

The government's new Care in the Community policy passes more responsibility to carers. From April 1993, local social services departments became responsible for assessing what help should be given to people, and making the necessary arrangements to deliver the service they need. By now, your social services department should have published details or you can ask your home help or social worker. Local voluntary bodies such as Age Concern, MIND, or a local carers' group should also be in the picture. A booklet setting out the new scheme and what is expected of it can be obtained free of charge. (See end for details.)

According to MIND, the national organisation for mental health, carers need:

- Recognition
- Respect
- Information
- Practical help
- Money
- Time Off
- Full implementation of the Disabled Persons Act 1986 and the Community Care Act 1990

Getting together with others helps in many ways – it gives people added muscle when lobbying for facilities, and relieves feelings to know others are in the same boat.

CHILDREN AND MENTAL ILLNESS

Children are bound to be affected if a parent is mentally ill. However, provided they are not at physical risk, they cannot and should not be shielded from reality. Answer their questions honestly, make sure they have enough of your time, and keep in close touch with school so that possible behavioural problems are understood there, and any warning signs passed on to you. Try to make time for lots of hugs to reassure your children that they are loved – that's what they most need to know. It will almost certainly be embarrassing for children, once they get to a certain age, to have a parent who is not "normal". It is easier for a child to deal with this kind of feeling if he/she can discuss it – don't make a parent's depression or other mental state a "no-go area" of conversation.

PRACTICAL STEPS

Seek reputable medical advice as soon as you can if your partner shows signs of suffering from mental distress. See the end of this book for some useful organisations or places to contact.

- Local carers' groups, voluntary organisations and helplines are there to offer support.

- Legal steps can be taken to protect you and your children if your partner ceases to be able to manage the family's affairs. A doctor can advise on an application to the Court of Protection to make you the receiver. These arrangements can be terminated when your partner has recovered. If a partner becomes violent, a treatment order can be obtained under Section 26 of the Mental Health Act.

TIME TO THINK

After the initial shock has worn off guilt and denial are common reactions to a partner's mental illness. Sweeping your own feelings under the carpet is only going to store up trouble for the future. Coming to terms with your partner's condition will take time. Many carers report that the change of personality in a loved one is the worst aspect of mental illness in a family. Feelings of powerlessness are hard to deal with. Mental and physical exhaustion are a carer's risk. Caring costs money – try to find time to work out the financial aspects of the family crisis.

2. ALZHEIMER'S DISEASE

THE PROBLEM

Alzheimer's disease – sometimes called senile dementia – affects millions of people in the world's ageing population. It can strike as early as 35, but most sufferers are over 65. When the disease occurs in people younger than 65, it is known as "early onset Alzheimer's disease". It is now believed that some of these sufferers are likely to have a family history of the disease. Researchers at St Mary's Hospital, London, demonstrated in 1990 that Alzheimer's disease is not a single disorder. They identified two types:

– an early onset form caused by genetic defects
– a late onset form caused by factors which may or may not be genetically linked

About 500,000 people altogether are estimated to be affected in Britain today. If they are living with someone, it is those people who have to care for them through the inexorable progress of the disease. Because it is a disease which affects mostly the elderly and because, statistically, women live longer than men, the carers for Alzheimer's sufferers are often elderly women whose hopes of a stress-free old age are cruelly eliminated, once the disease has been diagnosed. Alzheimer's differs from the ordinary forgetfulness of old age. Many old people have to be reminded of things. In advanced Alzheimer's sufferers it is as if the immediate past had never happened. Although the disease was identified over eighty years ago, its cause is not yet precisely known. Apart from the genetic element involved in the cases of younger ("early onset") sufferers, in other cases, an accident involving head injury or even a long operation seems to have triggered the onset of the disease. Because people are now living longer, the incidence of Alzheimer's is bound to grow. It is estimated that five per cent of pensioners will suffer from the disease.

THE WARNING SIGNS

Onset of Alzheimer's can be rapid or so gradual that it is thought to be absent-mindedness arising from stress. Often the family only recall the early signs of the disease after things have got considerably worse:

"He was gardening with me – he was always a very keen gardener. He's won prizes in shows. He started pulling out the flowers instead of the weeds."
(Harriet, 68, retired teacher)

"One evening he went to plug in the television and he couldn't get the plug in – he kept trying to put it in the wrong slot but he didn't seem to realise it."
(Emma, 72, retired nurse)

"His memory was getting worse and worse. It was driving me mad. We used to run a newsagent's but for the last few years I had to do all the ordering and the book-keeping – he just couldn't cope".
(Mary, 71, retired shop-keeper)

"They sent him home from a war exercise – he couldn't cope at all – they thought it was stress."
(Sara, 63, naval officer's widow)

"He gave one of his regular talks in the City – he was a very amusing speaker – and afterwards someone came up and said it wasn't as good as last year. He was very upset. I suppose it was because he knew something was going wrong."
(Martha, 54, investment adviser's widow)

"Just before he retired he went out and bought a pair of trousers and a jacket that were completely the wrong size."
(Honour, 77, wife of a painter/decorator)

Sometimes the disease seems to be triggered by an external event:

"He came round from the operation and suddenly couldn't tell the time."
(Felicity, 76, retired executive's wife)

FINDING OUT

When things get really bad a doctor is consulted:

"We thought it might be depression – he'd suffered from that in the past. The first time he went to the doctor's they said there was no sign of any shrinking of the cortex, so they ruled out Alzheimer's. Things didn't get any better – in fact they got considerably worse. I got very steamed up and went to see a psychiatrist. They did more tests at the Hospital for Nervous Diseases and that's when they found out."
(Harriet)

"I've been crucified by doctors. They were all so unhelpful. Nobody told me anything. I finally picked up a leaflet in the chemist's."
(Felicity)

"GPs aren't trained to deal with these people. The community psychiatric nurse – that's your best friend."
(Gina, 70, retired oil executive's wife)

"They still don't know whether he actually had Alzheimer's. The diagnosis still isn't brilliant. The only definite test is a post mortem. I couldn't face it. I felt he'd gone through enough . . ."
(Martha)

"They gave him a few question and answer tests and a brain scan. Then the doctor told me: it's Alzheimer's. I went away and tried to read up all I could."
(Honour)

Research is going on into any treatment which will halt the disease or prevent it. So far, no miracle drug or piece of genetic engineering has been discovered, although some hopeful leads are being pursued.

CARING BECOMES A FULL-TIME JOB

People suffering from Alzheimer's disease need constant care and crave company. They know it is going to get worse and are still sufficiently aware to show distress and insecurity. They follow their partner from room to room. The caring partner feels their emotions and their life have been turned upside down:

Strong Enough For Two

"He used to follow me round the house all the time. He was very quiet, I just looked round and there he was, right behind me."
(Martha)

"He was a terrific eater. But you had to be careful what you put on the table. He tried to eat some flowers and once I found him trying to eat my gloves."
(Sara)

"Love turns to hate. It doesn't last, this hate. You begin to hate them because they're completely opposite to what they were."
(Honour)

Sufferers can do embarrassing things. They go to the toilet on the floor and step in it; they wipe their dirty hands on the curtains; they go out into the street in their night clothes and say abusive words to passers-by.

"Time and time again I would have to say: he can't help it. Sometimes when he'd done something wrong, he would say that I had asked him to do it. They all seem to say that."
(Martha)

92

"I was frightened. Some people are frightened. A friend of mine used to lock herself into another bedroom at night."
(Harriet)

"The first couple of years your life is turned upside down. You're shattered. It takes about two years to come to terms with it."
(Honour)

LONELINESS, FRUSTRATION AND EXHAUSTION

Caring for an Alzheimer's partner is described sometimes as "watching little boxes close one after the other". As the disease takes its course, the sufferer ceases to be capable of carrying out even simple tasks.

"He used to help me with the washing-up. Then that stopped. I used to find things in the cupboard that he'd broken, carefully put together. Then he started having difficulty with words. He just didn't seem to be able to string them together. He would start off saying something and a lot of gobbledegook would come out."

"He could do tapestry at first, and stick pictures in an album – make a scrap book, that sort of thing.

Strong Enough For Two

Now he just sits. It's a twenty-four-hour-a-day thing. We don't go out anywhere without each other."
(Gina)

"The way I've heard it described best is: the lights are on, but there's no one at home."
(Harriet)

"However good your family is, you're still enclosed."
(Emma)

"At the beginning he could say: I'm just a bloody fool. You never knew whether you should explain to people what was the matter."
(Felicity)

Carers become exhausted from having night after night of broken sleep. The typical Alzheimer's patient gets up three or four times and has to be helped to the toilet. Sometimes they get up and get dressed in the middle of the night and have to be persuaded back to bed.

Feelings of stress are increased by a sense of having to cope alone:

"The doctor just said: you'll have to go home and make the best of it."
(Honour)

OUTINGS

In the early stages of their illness, Alzheimer's patients and their partners often enjoy going on outings, such as coach trips. The sufferer is kept safe from wandering and is distracted by the ever-changing views. The carer can relax for a few hours herself. Tragi-comic difficulties can arise when the sufferer needs to go to the toilet:

"There didn't used to be nearly enough toilets for the disabled – the sort where you can go in with him and help him. The number of times I stood outside the gents waiting for him. He'd go in and just not come out – he'd forgotten what he'd gone in for."
(Gina)

HOW LONG CAN YOU LOOK AFTER THEM?

The partner of an Alzheimer's sufferer is torn between wishing to keep and care for her loved one at home; and becoming discouraged, lonely and exhausted. Some carers find they cope better than they had feared. Others soon reach breaking point:

"A new psychiatric social worker was appointed just before my husband was due to be admitted to

long-term care. She started to argue about whether or not he was – I was – a deserving case. After all I'd been through I blew my top."
(Martha)

The Community Care Act 1990 requires every local authority to list individuals who have need of help, assess their need and draw up an individual plan for their care. One of the things that dementia carers value most highly is continuity of personnel. Another is flexible respite provision, so that a carer can have time off.

"The last time I left him in care was to go off and visit my daughter in America. I looked back and saw him sitting there with the others, and I thought: he's gone. He looked like all the other poor old buggers in the ward. I went back to the car and howled and howled."
(Harriet)

Funding is a problem in most regions of the country, whether for social services or long-term beds in hospitals. For the best up-to-date advice on getting the most you can for yourself and your partner, and every other issue affecting dementia sufferers and their families, contact the Alzheimer's Disease Society. (See back for details.)

ANXIETY AND DISTRESS

Both partners suffer from anxiety and distress. The Alzheimer's sufferer sometimes seems to be aware of what is happening:

"I found him crying in the bedroom. He said: I know what is happening to me."
(Harriet)

This level of insight, perhaps luckily, passes as the disease advances.

CASE STUDY: Anne and Andrew
Anne Wilson's husband, Andrew was diagnosed with Alzheimer's in 1989 when he was 41. He is an exceptionally young sufferer, and, as with many younger sufferers, his Alzheimer's is genetic in origin. His father and his aunt (his father's sister) died from the disease and his brother acquired it in his mid-thirties.

Mrs Wilson first detected signs of the disease when her husband was in his mid-thirties. It was originally diagnosed as depression over his bro-ther. A high-ranking army officer, Andrew was encountering problems at work as his memory was going.

Gradually he got worse. He was up every night,

couldn't find the loo, became incontinent, and grew more and more distressed. He also found it very upsetting to be taken anywhere for tests or check-ups, except when the ambulance picked him up because he thought he recognised the uniforms and was being picked up by an army bus.

Eventually he went into hospital for six weeks, and the nursing and psychotherapy were excellent. However, there were not enough long-term care beds and he had to return home. While he was in hospital, Anne realised that she could not carry on looking after him herself. Although it made her feel guilty – in many ways she feels that her 'job' is to care for her husband – a place has been found for him in a nursing home, and Anne visits him daily. She even enjoys having him at home for limited periods.

However, plans are afoot to close the nursing home. She is desperately campaigning against its closure, not knowing how she could cope otherwise.

Anne is thankful that they have no children in view of the genetic factor in her husband's condition. She is very concerned about the issue of younger people with Alzheimer's and the fact that there are limited resources available to them.

VIOLENCE AND ANGER

Alzheimer's sufferers sometimes become abusive or violent. They can lash out suddenly, especially if they misinterpret a movement:

"I was reaching for the kitchen paper and he must have thought I was going to do something to him – he just went like that with his arm and broke my glasses."
(Harriet)

"He used to say terrible things to our daughters. He didn't seem to know who they were."
(Honour)

"If I try to listen to the radio or have the TV on he sings at the top of his voice. It's me, me, me all the time. He wants my attention one hundred per cent. He used to take any piece of paper I wrote on, like shopping lists. I would find them in his clothes when I undressed him at night. It was if he wanted to hold on to part of me that way."
(Martha)

Carers can get violent and angry too when they are at the end of their tether:

99

"I used to say to him: I could kill you."
(Gina)

"We once had a girl in the group who had tried to strangle her mother who has Alzheimer's."
(Martha)

Carers are advised to step outside for "time out" or to ring for help when their feelings get the better of them.

MORE DIFFICULT TIMES: OBSESSIONS AND ISOLATION

Sometimes the Alzheimer's sufferer becomes convinced that his partner is going out of the house to see a lover. If he is at a day centre, he thinks that his partner (often now in the 80s) is going home to hold wild sex parties.

"It would be comical if it wasn't so sad. It really upsets my daughter. He simply goes on and on about my seeing other men."
(Gina)

Other sexual problems arise:

"It turned out he'd been interfering with the nurses at the home. They put him on a drug which toned that down anyway."
(Diana, 69, retired company director's wife)

Couples in which one partner suffers from Alzheimer's also suffer from social isolation:

"The children have got their lives to lead – I can't expect them to be round here all the time. Not when he's like this."
(Honour)

"My daughter used to get too upset to see her father. Before he died – before he got ill – he was such a bossy little man – the cock of the walk. She used to say: if Daddy knew what what was going to happen to him he would have shot himself."
(Sara)

An additional sadness for carers is the blight that the disease can inflict on their relationship with their adult children. The possibility that this incurable disease is hereditary can cause adult children extreme distress, which may be expressed in their staying away.

ALZHEIMER'S AND THE LAW

Because Alzheimer's affects a person's ability to deal with money and other every day business matters, it is useful to obtain an "Enduring Power of Attorney". This is a legal instrument designed to ensure that someone's affairs will be handled by a responsible individual, should they become mentally incapacitated. It must be arranged with the sufferer while they are still capable of giving consent. Many advisers suggest that everyone makes this arrangement while they are hale and hearty, because it makes life so much easier for carers in the event of the routine problems of old age, as well as any unexpected accidents. You could suggest that both of you make this arrangement, which may make it easier for a sufferer to accept. Other options which can come in useful include:

- Agency – a system whereby an individual undertakes to collect pensions and benefits on behalf of anyone who is mentally incapacitated.
- Appointeeship – the DSS can arrange for someone to receive and administer benefits on behalf of someone who is hospitalized or otherwise incapable of dealing with their own finances.
- Court of Protection – a receiver is appointed

under this system to deal with the sufferer's finances. If no one suitable can be found, the Court can appoint the Public Trustee to the role.
* Guardianship – a guardian decides where a person should live, advise on attendance for medical treatment, occupation and training and ensure that a doctor or social worker has access to the sufferer.

HELP IS AT HAND: GROUPS AND RESPITE

Belonging to a self-help group of other Alzheimer's sufferers' partners helps a lot:

"It was a chance to exchange stories. Everyone had a tale to tell. We laughed and cried together."
(Martha)

"Although my husband's now dead, I still run a club in my flat. It's nice and cosy and we're up to fifteen now. That's too many really. Everyone should get a chance once a week to have their say."
(Sara)

Local Alzheimer's groups can sometimes call on a "sitting service" which gives carers some respite. Respite care is available for, say, two weeks in every three months. The carer can get some rest without feeling they have abandoned their partner.

When the disease has reached a certain degree of severity, or the carer is unable to cope any longer, the patient can be taken into full-time care.

GRIEVING AND GUILT

The timing of an Alzheimer's patient being taken into permanent care is a matter of negotiation between the carer and the local social services (unless money is no object). The relief felt by an Alzheimer's sufferer's partner can be tinged with guilt and grief:

"You're grieving all the time whether you realise it or not. You feel very tired even when they've been taken into permanent care. You're in limbo really." (Harriet)

"They think you're hard. When he was taken ill the last time I said: please don't give him antibiotics." (Emma)

HOW IS IT GOING TO END?

"He wanted to kill himself. He couldn't find the words. He came in to me a few weeks before he died and said: would you put an end to it because I don't

know how. After that I started hiding the scissors
and the carving knife."
(Martha)

"At the end he went very quickly. I feel I've been one
of the lucky ones. It's usually pneumonia that takes
them off."
(Harriet)

"He'll end up as a vegetable. They all do. They just
look like skeletons at the end."
(Emma)

THE REWARD FOR CARING

Carers feel that they have been put in the situation
and coped as well as they could:

"You can't turn your back on it."
(Gina)

"We still loved each other – there's something to be
said for that after forty-seven years together. He told
me every day that he loved me."
(Sara)

"It's made me feel a stronger person for what I'm
going through now. I used to fall apart at bad news.

Now – I feel sorry but I keep together and that proves to me that I can cope."
(Emma)

TREATMENT POSSIBILITIES

CONVENTIONAL

Conventional medical research into Alzheimer's is going on in laboratories all over the world. Elaine Perry, a researcher in the field, says:

"Some of the drugs in development appear to retard the progress of the disease in some sufferers by one or two years, but there is still no prescribed treatment and certainly no cure. But because of the extent of the research effort, it would be reasonable to predict that drugs will be marketed within the next five to ten years."

ALTERNATIVE

Some people who think that they may be vulnerable to Alzheimer's because it seems to run in their family, have turned to homeopathic medicine. Homeopathic practitioner Charlotte Koelliker explains:

"Basically, homeopathy offers remedies to deal with many of the symptoms characteristic of Alzheimer's. Obviously, it is difficult to make any changes once

106

brain tissue and systems have become damaged, but if you start early enough you can prevent deterioration to a great extent. Homeopathy treats the individual. Where conventional medicine tends to look for common symptoms, what interests us is what individualises a condition. Conventional medicine tends to hold a mechanistic view of the body: if it's dead, cut it out. We think that given the right stimulus, it's extraordinary how bodies can regenerate. You have to look at a person's life. A lot of old people just shut down. If you can prevent that you can restore quite a reasonable amount of function. It's difficult but it's not hopeless – so long as the life force is still there."

Homeopathy can offer treatment for loss of identity and loss of memory and also offers medication if a person has lapsed into a childish state.

Homeopathy can also offer relief to carers:

"The symptoms we would be looking for in a carer of an Alzheimer's sufferer, and that we would seek to treat, would be such things as the effects of prolonged night watching, grief, and suppressed anger."

Homeopaths can be doctors registered under the aegis of the Association of Homeopaths, or practitioners belonging to the professional Society of

Homeopaths, or alternatively belonging to the UK Homeopathic Medical Association. If a carer wishes to explore other alternatives to conventional medicine, they could contact the Institute of Complementary Medicine. Costs per consultation range from £25 to £60. (See back for further details.)

PHYSICAL ILLNESS

Part Three

PHYSICAL ILLNESS

WHEN A PARTNER'S HEALTH FAILS

Physical health is something most people take for granted until something goes wrong. Overnight, a doctor's diagnosis or an accident can totally change people's lives. Physical illness can be terminal or curable, short or long term. Whichever is the case, when a person is ill, a partner is bound to feel the strain. The everyday experience of caring for someone who is just suffering a bout of flu, shows how many small extra demands can increase a carer's burden to breaking point. Apart from the immediate practical problems such as laundry, ferrying food up and down stairs and dashing to the chemist, there is mental strain. People in physical pain can be irritable and demanding. The well partner may feel anxious, guilty and angry. In a relationship where the sick partner has previously taken his full share of the responsibility for the running of the household, his absence from active participation is keenly felt.

CASE HISTORY: Gertrude and Taylor

Gertrude and Taylor had been married a year when he "just stopped walking" one Monday morning. Gertrude explains: *"It was something quite rare, called a spinal angioma. It is a hereditary condition which affects the blood vessels leading to the spinal cord."* The condition had begun to manifest itself some six months previously, when Taylor, a brilliant research scientist then aged 30, began to complain of back pain. At the time, Gertrude was 28.

To complicate things even further Gertrude had just given birth to their first (and only) child. Penny – now aged 26 – was only three weeks old when Taylor collapsed, and the young family had also just moved into a house on a new housing estate. *"The house was so new that we weren't even on the telephone"* says Gertrude. *"I can't remember now how we got hold of a doctor."* In the first three days Taylor was moved to three different hospitals. Finally the National Hospital for Nervous Diseases in Maida Vale, London, identified the source of the problem and undertook an emergency operation, to relieve pressure on his spine and restore the blood supply, without which Taylor would have died. Three months later another operation was attempted, to repair the damage to his spine, but this time he suffered cardiac arrest.

The surgeon managed to get Taylor's heart restarted and rang Gertrude while Taylor was still unconscious in Intensive Care. *"He said to me with typical dry Scots understatement: 'We've had a rather busy day. You'd better come up'*," remembers Gertrude. It was feared that Taylor might have suffered brain damage (because he had effectively "died" during the operation) on top of the paralysis and might never recover consciousness.

"Taylor scarcely saw Penny for the first three months of her life. She spent most of her infanthood lying in the back of our Landrover being fed a bottle at totally unsuitable temperatures. That whole time I was so bloody tired that when I went to bed I just went out like a light. One just got on with it. You had to. What else was there to do?"

Gertrude's parents lived sixty miles away and had day-to-day commitments that were hard to drop, but Taylor's parents came to the rescue. *"His father was particularly wonderful in those first few months. And one of our new neighbours turned up trumps."*

After three months, Taylor was sent to Roehampton for rehabilitation. *"In those days Roehampton was very much the ex-military hospital. There was a wonderful sister in charge – Sister Heal. The first evening Taylor was there I came to visit and she boomed, 'Have you brought a bottle with you?' It turned out that her regular prescription for her 'boys' in the evenings was a drop of whisky. The dear old colonel in the bed next door who had had a leg amputated produced his bottle that first night, and we all had a drink on him. Sister Heal gave me the best piece of advice I had from anyone. She said: 'Don't make any allowances. He's still the same person, you know.' As a result, I treat him exactly as I did before the illness. People might even think that I'm beastly to him sometimes. Penny was very protective towards him even when she was little. They're still very close. When she was crawling, she would never tease him by going out of reach if I'd left them together and gone out to the shops or something. She obviously realised that he had physical limitations. But in some ways it was an advantage – it gave her social cachet as a child. She was heard to boast at children's parties: 'My daddy's got a wheelchair'."*

Taylor is paraplegic – paralysed in both legs. He was lucky, because he was already employed by a university college in central London when illness struck, and they immediately offered the family accommodation in college a ten-minute wheelchair push on the level from his teaching block.

"The difference between us and a 'normal' couple is that everything takes longer – and costs more. For instance, it takes time and planning to get anywhere. It takes time to get in and out of the car. You cannot use public transport, and can only use certain sorts of cab. Inside the flat, it takes time to manoeuvre the wheelchair around obstacles if Taylor is laying the table or washing up. If I go away for

the night, I have to remember to leave things where he can reach them – food and clothes, that sort of thing." The problem of storing things out of reach affects the disabled who share a house with able-bodied partners more, perhaps, than those who live alone and can design their whole way of life around their reach from a wheelchair.

The expense of being paraplegic includes motoring: *"We always have to have our car modified with hand throttle and brake controls – that costs around £800. Also, whenever we go away for conferences or on holiday we have to correspond for ages with hotels, checking and re-checking that they are 'wheelchair friendly'. Two out of ten that claim to be simply aren't when you get there."* On one famous occasion in New York the receptionist was asked if there were any stairs *"up to the restaurant"* and she assured them that there weren't. When they got there, there were stairs. *"Oh yes,"* said the receptionist blithely, *"there are stairs* down *to the restaurant"* . . . A counterbalance is provided by the state disability allowance, currently split between mobility at £11.55 per week, attendance at £43.35 and living at £28.95 per week – a total of £83.85."

Taylor and Gertrude have neighbours who can come in in an emergency and their GP lives three doors away. This was very useful last year when Taylor became very ill with septicaemia. (Septicaemia is when an infection in one part of the body begins to affect the bloodstream, which carries the infection to other parts of the body and can quickly result in death.) *"It made me realise how important pain is. Taylor has no pain sensation in parts of his body so he was not able to signal where the trouble was. He lost weight and didn't look well for a while – we thought it was overwork and then he suddenly became very ill."*

On the ups and downs of her own ability to cope, Gertrude says: *"I tend to be very self-contained. Obviously one has the occasional day when one is fed up. For instance, not long ago my mother became senile – unable to cope on her own any longer. We asked our doctor over and told him all our woes over a bottle of claret. And when Taylor was so ill last year, our doctor used to ring me first thing every morning and ask: 'How are you today?' It's much easier to cope with a physical disability than to watch someone you know deteriorate mentally – change into another person. The most upsetting thing I found about my mother was not knowing how much she was aware of what was going wrong. I'm fortunate that it's the 'same old Taylor'. Our marriage has worked mostly because of the sort of person Taylor is. A friend of mine was married to a man who became crippled through polio. He was belligerently independent – impossibly so. Taylor is quite happy to be helped around the house. If he needs help he asks for it. What he dreads are well-meaning ladies in hats who come up behind him when he is wheeling himself merrily along, and just take charge of the chair – start pushing it along without so much as a by your leave. The best thing is if people just say: are you OK or do you need a hand? How you get on depends so much on the disabled person. If he becomes bitter it's much more of a strain. Disability brings out the best and the worst in people – it underlines traits that you already have. Taylor has done quite a bit in his time for the disabled, sat on various committees such as the Disabled Living Foundation and so on. Now he feels he can hand over to a younger generation (he is 57). On the whole we do not seek out other disabled couples – rather the opposite."*

SEVERE ILLNESS

A breakdown in physical health may happen suddenly or it may be gradual. A heart attack or stroke often happens out of the blue:

"He had had an ordinary day, really. He had been out playing golf in the afternoon. He drove up outside the house, parked the car and came in and said he felt dizzy and a bit sick. There was pain going down both his arms. I called an ambulance

while he sat in the hall. They told me later that he had had a massive heart attack. He was in Intensive Care."
(Mary, 48, graphic artist)

"I didn't realise to begin with how serious it was. It was lambing time and he was working one morning out in the shed. He was rushed to hospital and operated on immediately: he had a ruptured aorta."
(Camilla, 42, farmer's wife)

A doctor's diagnosis of a terminal health problem is a shock:

"Martin had been feeling – and looking – terrible. He finally agreed to go and see the doctor. They did some tests and called us in. The doctor said: it's cancer of the liver."
(Patricia, 37, writer)

In some cases, serious physical illness can creep up gradually: in motor neurone disease, for example, the person can continue to feel vaguely unwell and unfit for months, attributing symptoms to minor illnesses. The world-famous scientist and author Dr Stephen Hawking (now almost totally paralysed by MN) has described how his condition was finally identified, when he fell over whilst skating and found he simply couldn't get up. According to him, his wife was extremely influential in willing him to live when doctors pronounced him likely to die.

Accidents at work or injury in a road accident are equally traumatic. In these cases, you do not even have the minimal preparation of knowing your partner has been "off colour". The news is sudden and frightening. A person goes into reactive mode, on "automatic pilot":

"A policeman came to the door and said: 'I'm afraid there's been an accident.' Tim had been riding his bike back from work and there was a collision with a truck. Your mind just goes blank from the shock."
(Rosemary, 32, florist)

"The friend who had been with him in the car when the accident happened rang me from hospital. I can't remember what I thought. I was in total shock. I just sat down and trembled. I just did what had to be done and sorted things out afterwards."
(Angela, 27, librarian).

Sometimes, the after-effects of hearing shocking news are very serious. A lot of research has been carried out on post-trauma stress, and the results show that people who appear to cope well at the time of an accident, can experience bad dreams and anxiety attacks for months or even years after the event.

WHAT HAPPENS NOW?

News that your partner is gravely ill and likely to remain so takes time to sink in.

"I was absolutely numb. I just drove myself home from the hospital in shock. I discovered when I got home that he had got the keys to the lambing shed in his pocket, so someone – not me, thank goodness – had to rush back for them because all the sheep were in there and lambing started that night. I didn't even have the telephone number of the contract shepherd he had booked to help him."
(Camilla)

Having to cope with the immediate problems – contacting your partner's family and workplace, arranging transport to and from hospital, dealing with children's questions – is in some ways a relief. Being so busy provides a short-term cushion against the harder issues to address in the longer term.

"It was a nightmare – decisions, decisions, decisions. But in a way, it helps to take your mind off the other worry: will he ever get better – really better?"
(Rosemary)

GETTING BETTER SLOWLY

If your partner has a serious heart operation or a stroke, he may get better slowly. Your partner may worry that he will not be the same mentally or physically:

"After his operation, which was a success from the physical point of view, he did seem so different. He had forgotten a lot. I worried that he was never going to be the same. It took a long time to adjust, but of course you do. After all, the alternative is him being dead, isn't it?"
(Jilly, 38, housewife and mother)

"William had a stroke when he was only 45. He lost his speech and all movement down one side to begin with. He's got better very very slowly, and now we realise he is never going to recover completely. But the experience hasn't been all negative. You discover things about yourself and your partner that you never would otherwise."
(Jane, 48, legal executive)

CASE HISTORY: Caroline and Harry
Caroline's husband had a stroke ten years ago, when he was 60. *"We had had a very busy time. It was the company's Year End which always meant Harry had a*

lot of extra work, and we'd also been organising a big charity event. At about 6.00p.m. that Saturday, he said he wasn't feeling well and was going to bed. He woke up around 2.00a.m. and couldn't speak. For some reason I had it stuck in my head that it must be something to do with the fact that the walls of his study had been newly painted, and the strong smell of paint must have affected him. I called the doctor and he said that it was probably a slight stroke. Harry had lost movement down his right side.

I remember thinking 'It'll be all right, we're members of BUPA' which is pretty absurd, but you do think absurd things in moments of crisis. He was taken to hospital, but I still wasn't too worried. The next day he got worse and then he went into a coma.

I cannot tell you how badly I think I was treated. I am a practising lawyer and I was simply stunned by the lack of communication during the whole episode. Eventually the hospital rang me at work and said: 'You should feel free to come in any time.' I wanted to get hold of the consultant but whenever I tried I was fobbed off. He was busy. In the end I had to phone his wife at home to make an appointment.

I took my eldest daughter with me and she asked the consultant if Harry was going to die. The consultant said that he was, and when I asked if he had ever seen anyone recover from this state I remember his words exactly: 'Yes, but it happens so rarely, it is etched on my memory.'

Physical Illness

The worst thing was having to tell my two other children. We had an American lawyer friend visiting who was tremendous. She got food, took the children for walks, and was there to listen.

Then, a week after everything had begun, I walked into the ward and, lo and behold! Harry was sitting up in bed, his eyes open. From then on he got better, although he was in and out of hospital for months. I couldn't believe he'd pulled through. I had considered him dead – the hope had gone. I'd even planned his funeral. Harry remembers nothing of that week.

Then I had to face the tremendous practical problems. Harry's business affairs had to be sorted out. I am a partner in a City law firm. My colleagues were very understanding for about two weeks, and then forgot about it as other problems cropped up. Meanwhile I visited Harry in hospital twice a day, and had to look after the children alone.

People's reactions were interesting. Some didn't know how to help; some just didn't want to get involved; and some were just incredibly insensitive. On the other hand, one neighbour just said 'I've made supper for all of you and put it in the fridge'. And one day I was shopping when someone who lives in our village stopped me and asked if I would like her to be a full-time housekeeper – cook the meals, collect the children, take the youngest to Brownies, etc.

Harry got well enough to come home but he could do virtually nothing. The improvement was slow, very slow. He reached a plateau after three and a half years. Now he's terribly sleepy and, somehow, a different person. He suffers from mild epilepsy which is kept under control with medication. His right arm is quite useless but he's learned to do some things with the left. We've had rails put round the house to help him. I was angry and sad – predominantly sad.

In many ways it's made us closer. Maybe we had been growing apart – I'm thirteen years younger than he is, and he was drinking a lot at the time of the stroke. Now we do a lot of things together – for instance I read to him or we play backgammon.

It's very frustrating – ordinary outings are more difficult, although disabled facilities are much better than they were when we first needed them. Luckily we have always been secure financially, but now I am the only breadwinner, and there is pressure on me to continue earning although retirement looms.

Life will go on. I'm happy 70 per cent of the time. It's odd really, talking about it after so long."

CARING FOR CHILDREN

Children notice when things go wrong. A parent's illness will affect children of all ages. Evidence of a parent's vulnerability, and indeed mortality, is a significant event in all children's lives. Young children are very adaptable but need reassurance through reminders that they matter too. They may hesitate to ask questions in case they cause more upset, or the answers confirm their worst fears. The best solution is to talk and encourage children to do the same. Silence or brushing off awkward questions is going to store up trouble in the future. Do not shy away from the big issues. For instance a child may say: "Is Daddy going to die?" You should answer truthfully. Younger children can be encouraged to express their emotions by painting or acting out their fears in play.

"Tell school what is going on, so that teachers understand why there may be episodes of difficult behaviour. When children are worried they often act it out, they can start bullying another child or they may become very withdrawn."
(Romy, 45, hospice counsellor)

It is important to make "quality time" for children. Their life is ticking away inexorably, too. Life is not a rehearsal for anyone of any age, and children cannot be put on hold.

"He said: tell the children I'm going to die. We both of us felt it was better to tell the truth from the outset."
(Patricia)

Children may be going through a natural period of growing up and away. Young adults often experience a period of needed separation from their parents, to establish their own autonomy before being able to "make friends" again. A serious illness can make them feel intensely guilty that they are doing this.

"In some ways it helped that I had been married before and had had to cope on my own with four children before I married Michael. I had learned a certain sort of independence."
(Camilla)

"To a certain extent, you live from day to day. With a progressive illness, things can go along quite well for a while, then there's a setback. You can't plan far ahead at all, really."
(Susan, 31, computer programmer)

Adult children may be more affected than anyone realises by the illness of a parent. Make sure they get time alone with you both.

DON'T FORGET YOUR NEEDS

A carer can become swamped with others' needs. Give yourself time and space. No one is inexhaustible.

126

"Getting away from time to time is important. To begin with, I didn't want to go away even for the weekend. Then after a particularly difficult period when I had been really stressed physically and mentally, I realised I had to have a break – for both our sakes."
(Camilla)

"You can forget that you need looking after too from time to time. Having someone who depends on you for most of their needs is very exhausting."
(Patricia)

"I go to this church where they have a meeting place behind the altar. They invite anyone who wants help to come round after communion. It's all very discreet. Volunteer counsellors are there to pray or talk with people who are in distress or anxious or under some particular pressure. There is something about being still and quiet with our thoughts and with God that I find very helpful."
(Camilla)

GUILT, ANGER AND FEAR

It is normal to experience a mixture of emotions when a loved one is taken seriously ill or is disabled. Loving concern is bound to be mixed with other less easily accepted emotions. There may be anger: why did he let me down? Why *my* partner? Fear is also natural – and worry about what the future holds. There may be bitterness and regret about opportunities which now seem to have gone for ever. A person experiences the realisation that things can never be the same.

"I sometimes regret all the things we put off. We used to say: we'll go off and see such-and-such – Venice, say, – when the children are older. Now we'll never be able to do them together."
(Angela)

"We had a silly row the morning he was taken ill. It was just a stupid thing. He'd said something about the sunrise being so beautiful and I pretended not to hear because I was cleaning my teeth. He stumped off and of course the next thing I knew they were saying he'd been taken so ill . . ."
(Camilla)

COPING WITH EMOTIONS

Emotions should not be bottled up. Most people understand that physical illness in a family puts physical, mental and emotional strain on everyone, but especially on you, the main carer. Sometimes, people can be unlucky – they find that professionals are too busy to talk to them about their worries.

There are various other ways to share the load: friends, church, a group of people in similar situations, relations.

"I go to creative writing classes once a week. It takes my mind off home completely for a while, and I have a programme of reading which helps in the evenings."
(Patricia)

"It's physically very tiring. He goes into a respite home for two weeks in every six. My biggest problem has been doctors. I've really had to battle for the last two years."
(Verity, 60, husband suffering from stroke and incontinence)

GETTING INTO EQUILIBRIUM

Gradually everyone comes to terms with the new situation. There may even be unexpected "pluses". Facing difficult times together can be a bond. Recurrent episodes of anger or frustration are easier to deal with because they have been recognised and dealt with before. A carer knows that "bad" days and "good" days happen.

"It can change in the blink of an eyelid. He goes up and down. Some days he can do stairs, some days he can't."
(Verity)

TALKING ABOUT DYING

Most people at some stage of their lives – regardless of special circumstances, such as having a chronically ill partner – begin to get to grips with the idea of life coming to an end. An episode of ill health or the onset of a chronic illness brings this process to the fore. A fear of death can express itself in unexpected ways – people may try to deal with it through denial.

"He started to hurry through things as if he was catching some imaginary train all the time. It was getting ridiculous. I went to the doctor and he said: because of his heart trouble, he is probably aware of death for the first time. Some people fend off the prospect of death by becoming terribly over-organised and meticulous – also, making yourself incredibly busy all the time is his way of avoiding thinking the unthinkable."
(Miranda, 39, lawyer)

THINKING ABOUT THE FUTURE

After the immediate crisis is over, you have time to think about longer term practical and emotional issues:

- Finance – if a partner's earnings are going to be affected, what impact will that have on your family budget? Now is the time for both of you to make a will, if you have not already done so, or to look again at your existing wills.
- Household management – if your partner is likely to spend more time in bed or have difficulty in using stairs, assess the suitability of your house. It is often possible – even preferable – to adapt an existing house rather than move. Moving is a trauma in itself, and you will need all your existing support systems in the shape of neighbours and friends when your partner is ill.

"I didn't have the faintest idea how to do things like insure the car, for example. He had done all that sort of thing before the accident."
(Angela)

How do you think about the future when a partner is physically unwell or disabled? Tips from those who have lived for a long time with a partner in poor health:

"Well, you can do things like plan not to live too far from the services you're bound to need – doctors and hospitals, that sort of thing. We had been thinking of moving to the country but basically that got shelved when Martin got ill."
(Anthea, 47, craft shop proprietor)

"We plan treats – nothing too elaborate and nothing too far ahead. It helps us both to have things to look forward to."
(Camilla)

"Having our first grandchild was a tremendous boost. You can't exactly plan for that yourselves, but I suppose the great thing is that it gives you the feeling that life is going to go on – you know, after you've gone."
(Verity)

ACCEPT HELP

"It's far more helpful if people offer something specific rather than just saying: let me know if there is anything I can do." (Mary, husband was in Intensive Care).

THINGS THAT PEOPLE COULD DO TO HELP A PERSON "TAKING THE STRAIN"
(guidelines you could give if help is offered)

- bring presents of ready-made food dishes
- do the shopping
- take the children out
- do the washing/ironing
- pass on messages giving an up-to-date progress bulletin to friends and family – it gets very exhausting for the partner to do it all herself
- walk the dog
- ring up on a regular day and ask how things are going – and listen
- give the carer a little treat – bath oil or some gourmet delicacy – to cheer her up

"It is a shock, when you think you are a capable middle-aged woman, to find suddenly that you need to stop and be looked after yourself."
(Jilly)

MAINLY MONEY

Part Four

MAINLY MONEY

WHY MONEY CAN CAUSE SUCH STRIFE

In any relationship, money plays an important role. Partners are very often chosen for their earning power. Women today are carrying a greater and greater share of the day-to-day responsibilities for earning and managing the family's finances. Many relationships threaten to founder over money. Financial stresses and strains can cause health and emotional problems to arise within a relationship.

One relatively new group are couples ruined by Lloyd's losses. Many of these are retired people who now find themselves with severe money worries, when they expected to live out their lives in comfort – and leave something to their children.

"My husband began to realise a couple of years ago that he had very bad losses. He's become very depressed – it's undermined his health completely. It's the worry of the unknown. There are debts which we'd never have been able to repay. It's just been fear and worry, fear and worry. He's been seeing a psychiatrist. It's affected his sleep and his

137

eating. He's on anti-depressants but he gets into such a slough of despair. He just doesn't seem to want to do anything – he used to play bowls and bridge. Now we just stay at home. Luckily we have been accepted by the Hardship Fund. They take everything you've got left, but they allow you enough to live on while the 'name' (the member of Lloyd's, in this case the husband) is alive. I don't know what is going to happen to me when he dies – I don't think they do either."

(Betty, 71, married to a Lloyd's "name")

In other cases, following the yuppy boom and bust of the 1980s, your partner may have earned too much too soon and too easily – and then lost his job.

"We had been living it up – we had bought our own flat and lots of nice things to go in it. We ate out all the time – I did virtually no cooking for the first few years we were married. Tim's job as a currency dealer in a bank was the absolute mainstay of our existence. Then it all fell apart . . . and I ended up carrying the marriage for four or five years."

(Felicity, 35, interior designer).

According to Simon Johnson of National Debtline, it is often the woman in a partnership who not only accepts the need for help, but will actually contact an agency such as his for advice – and then be the one who undertakes the lengthy negotiations with creditors to resolve the debt problem:

"Women are usually willing to discuss their problems frankly and be guided by one of our advisers."

Even those who seem to have been lucky financially can have problems:

"People kept telling me how lucky I was, but inheriting money is a two-edged sword. In some ways it holds you back because you don't have the same incentive as others to better yourself. My husband didn't bother to work because he knew that when the chips were down, I could pay the bills."
(Georgina, 35, journalist)

Women increasingly resent giving up a well-paid career to have children:

"When I was working, I was earning twice as much as my husband. Now we have a baby and we're living on his salary I can't get used to having to scrimp and save. The worst part is having to depend on him for everything we spend."
(Serena, 27, investment analyst)

139

During periods of recession many people think that increased money worries are to blame for the break-up of relationships and marriages. However, professional RELATE counsellors say that, contrary to what many people might expect, in a recession the number of relationships where money troubles are reported to be the main bone of contention, remains more or less the same in proportion to all other causes of tension. Renate Olins, of London RELATE rejects the common view that money troubles *by themselves* are to blame for marriage or relationship breakdown:

"Of course, the recession is an added strain and to lose your job is very upsetting and impoverishing. This problem forces a review of lifestyles. It strengthens the relationship of some couples. They view the recession rather like the war: it provides a common cause for them to rally round.

However, if a relationship is ailing and a cataclysmic blow falls, those couples feel they can't struggle on. But splitting up makes the financial problems worse."

Psychologist Dr Paul Webley of Exeter University has studied the question of how money interacts with relationships:

"A shortage of money exacerbates unresolved conflicts which are, underneath, more to do with ideas of power and possession and man/woman responsibilities than

money itself. So, in a recession, more people are having to confront these underlying problems which were previously smoothed over and camouflaged, when there was plenty of money to go around."

Very often, a man's self-esteem and feeling of power in a relationship is bound up with his being the main provider. Some couples may not even realise this – they have a joint bank account and use the rhetoric of equality. However, when he loses his job, for instance and has to rely on his partner for support, he finds his self-esteem shattered.

CASE HISTORY: Barbara and Richard
Barbara and Richard were both teachers when they met. Soon after their marriage they moved south to be near her parents.

After a couple of years Richard decided he wanted to try his hand at running his own business. Initially, he planned to design and market teaching aids from their spare bedroom. Then he decided that, since he had no experience of running a business, he would do better to buy a quick printing franchise.

Barbara had inherited money and they used some of this to buy their printing business. Unfortunately it was the beginning of the recession. As the local economy got worse, so margins tightened until they were faced with their first really hard decision – to give up the business after barely a year's trading or plunge into further expense with a superior colour copier to give them the edge over their local competitors. They decided to 'go for broke'.

Financially things went from bad to worse. Richard started refusing to discuss any details of the business with her, even though it was her capital which they had invested in it. They remortgaged their house. *"The stronger I appeared to be, the worse things got but if I ever complained he would heap scorn on me,"* Barbara remembers. *"There came a point when I couldn't even talk about the situation with my closest friends.*

Richard started using amphetamines to keep himself going during the day and marijuana to calm himself down again in the evening. I felt sick all the time. Home was not a place to go to relax and be safe, it was a battleground. There was nowhere to hide."

In her effort to keep her ailing marriage afloat, Barbara got pregnant again, but when Richard reacted with fury she realised her mistake. *"I started going to marriage guidance at that point,"* she says. *"I went on my own once a week throughout the pregnancy and for two months after Tom was born. I kept on saying to myself*

'I've got to make this work,' but finally, when Tom was 18 months old I told Richard I'd had enough.

It wasn't the business failure as such, but his attitude to it that broke our marriage. He never, ever listened to me. He couldn't share his worries, he could only take them out on me or the children. He was a fine person to have around when everything was going well. Perhaps if his morale had been higher he might have agreed to go to counselling.

We should have separated long before we actually did. The children are only just coming out of their shells now, two years later. I had only been keeping the marriage going for their sakes, and then I realised Richard's behaviour was having a very detrimental effect on them."

Barbara realises that she was lucky. She had supportive friends and family. Her parents helped her to get back on her feet again, and encouraged her to achieve a measure of reconciliation with Richard, so that the children were not deprived of access to their father. *"I was left to sort out the whole business with the bank. The bank manager had been an absolute bastard. He had known that I had some capital, so he had encouraged Richard to borrow more and more regardless of the fact the monthly figures clearly showed he was continuing to trade at a loss. In the end I had to sell the house to pay off the debts. I used up all my inheritance, but at least I was free.*

The advice I'd give to anyone in my situation is that you can't trust anyone – especially not professional advisers. Bank managers, estate agents, lawyers – none of them give a damn about you. It's every man for himself."

OUT OF CONTROL . . . AND SINKING?

Being out of control of money is particularly frightening. It helps if couples are able to share money worries, but often they do not.

"The fact that the business was failing – we were losing money hand over fist and our house was on the line – was a complete no-go area. He refused to discuss it, although I begged him to. He just didn't want to discuss it – full stop."
(Mandy, 28, primary school teacher)

"Tim just hid his head in the sand when he lost his job. I discovered that he hadn't been paying any tax on his earnings. Tim disappeared to the golf course. I had to deal with the tax man, and keep things going generally."
(Felicity).

"It's rather like coming across a road accident. You get into top gear and you cope."
(Rose, 38, property manager)

144

"For a while after he was made redundant, he was impossible to talk to. That's what was the most difficult thing to bear – we were still married, but I felt as though I was on my own."
(Karen, 36, EFL teacher)

"George was so proud of his job. He identified totally with the firm. When they closed his division, it was as if he had lost a member of the family. He grieved – as though someone had died."
(Penny, 41, housewife)

ALL IN THE SAME BOAT

In a recession, there is some consolation in knowing that many other people are experiencing the same stomach-churning sensations when a letter arrives from the bank manager or the building society. The old stigma attached to bankruptcy and repossession has lessened. However, like many bad things in life, it may have seemed that "it couldn't happen to us". But it can. And maybe now it has. Worse, if your partner has become bogged down in his financial plight then you may have to step in.

"What made it worse was that he had always talked about people who got into money troubles as if it was somehow their own fault. But when you have a

145

mortgage and you lose your job and you can't get another one, it isn't exactly bad management is it – so many people round us are in the same situation."
(Rose)

Debtors feel intimidated and powerless.

"We never realised that we could complain to anyone about harassing calls from creditors or that the County court helps both sides."
(Felicity)

CASE HISTORY: Annette and David
Annette thought she was comfortably settled for life, with a beautiful Georgian house in Berkshire and a holiday flat in Marbella. Her husband, David, was a high-flyer with a City merchant bank. He worked very long hours, sometimes through the weekend, but then so did many of Annette's friends' husbands.

"I knew vaguely that he was working on some terribly big deal," she says. *"But of course he could never discuss details of his work with me at home, because everything had to be kept absolutely confidential until whatever the deal was had been put together."* The "big deal" her husband was working on was a share issue which, through no fault of his, was badly timed.

"He came home one evening at about 10.30p.m."

146

says Annette. *"I'll never forget the look on his face. He looked as though he was sleep-walking. I think he knew exactly how things were going to go from then on. Scandal in the City is a bit like having AIDS,"* says Annette. *"It was unbelievable how quickly the rumours spread. People who had known us for years dropped us long before anything became publicly known. It was incredibly painful . . ."*

To make matters worse, her husband became obsessed with his own defence. The case was long and complicated and related litigation stretched ahead forever. It soon became clear that their capital was going to be swallowed up in legal costs, even if he were to clear his name. *"We were in a completely no-win situation. David knew that even if the court cleared him, he would never get back into the City inner circle where he had been before. It's a place where you don't ever get a second chance."*

Financially, Annette and David had to face some hard facts. They had been living up to the hilt of his generous salary and bonuses. Now he was "on leave" from the bank. Money continued to flood out but the prospect of endless litigation stretched ahead. *"He had the house put in my name so that if he went bankrupt we would not lose that. The flat in Marbella was put on the market but, of course, it was the beginning of the recession, although we did not realise that at the time. The flat stayed on the market for two years until it was finally sold for only one third of what we paid for it in 1988.*

It wasn't so much losing our lifestyle which really got to me," says Annette. *"It was losing our marriage. David was always very ambitious, almost frighteningly so. He just had to win at everything. When this happened, he was really destroyed. He became someone I didn't really know. To be honest, I found it difficult to like him. He was totally self-obsessed. The children (then aged 13 and 15) had to be quiet all the time when they were in the house. School holidays were a nightmare . . ."*

CRISIS LOOMS

Depression, anxiety and aggressive behaviour may be the result of money worry. Your partner may become excessively secretive, hide letters that come recorded delivery in ominous and increasingly familiar brown envelopes, start to drink, have an affair. You may feel angry at being left to cope with the mess, but on the other hand, feel it is a relationship worth preserving. Most people will look for someone to blame in a time of crisis. Someone under great stress due to financial worries, will put the blame on the person closest to hand – his partner. When for instance you are criticised for spending money on absolute essentials, it is difficult not to feel angry and isolated. And there are further complications. Your affairs are inextricably linked – people share a house as well as a bed. There may be children to consider. Now there is a financial crisis to share.

WHO'S IN CHARGE?

In this situation a woman feels she is walking on eggs. The rows increase. The criticism of her grows, and various discoveries are made. The money from the joint account that was going to pay the mortgage has been paying off business debts, the house and its contents are no longer insured. Then things go beyond the point where any partner is prepared to stand back. The collision with disaster seems too obvious. Someone has to take the reins.

"Every time I started asking him about the business and the money we owed, he would lose his temper. But one day I just said to him: You've got to tell me exactly where we stand financially. Once it was out in the open, he kind of collapsed like a pricked balloon. It was almost as if once he had told me exactly how bad things were, it was no longer his responsibility. He just left me to get on with it and start to sort out the mess."
(Bridget, 53, office manager/financial controller)

In some cases women feel they should have moved quicker:

"He used to lie if I asked him about the situation. Looking back, I now think that I should have insisted on being more involved from the start. He wanted to prove he could go it alone, but that wasn't a very good basis for a small family business."
(Barbara)

CRISIS TIME

A) TAKING OVER
There are two kinds of crisis and basically they require two sorts of response. Curiously enough, many people find that once the decision is made to takeover the situation completely, they possess an amazing amount of calm. It can be a gradual takeover or one that is complete in one fell swoop. Do not expect your partner to be grateful. Not only must it be done with verve, it must also be done with tact. Your partner is grey and haggard, suffering from the cumulative effects of months of sleepless nights. He doesn't seem to be able to think rationally about the situation any longer, and there is a fear that he may collapse completely under the strain of it all. It becomes clearer and clearer to you

that for a while you are going to have to take charge.

"I remember looking at him and thinking: I wouldn't let a dog go on suffering like that. So I just picked up the phone and made an appointment to see our bank manager myself. I was totally determined and to my amazement – it worked."
(Rose)

B) BEING AN ANCHOR
Many women assume the responsibilities for a while to "stand by their man". Others give up their careers to help:

"I had been working very happily for a friend as office manager/financial controller of a small service company. When J's business showed signs of failing I felt I had to go to the rescue. I had some capital invested, which was one consideration. He had never wanted me to be too closely involved on a day-to-day basis. So in a way it was a great sacrifice of his principles when I came in and took over the paperwork and administration. There was no other alternative: he couldn't afford to employ anyone, and he couldn't both be out selling and man the office."
(Bridget)

151

According to Renate Olins, the issue really is: can a man allow himself to step back and accept his partner in her changed role? In a lot of cases it's an enormous emotional problem. For the majority of men it's a very difficult thing to come to terms with – there is a sexual threat. These issues "rock the boat". For most couples, the key to success is the way they work out that shift in power.

HELP IS AT HAND

A) OBVIOUS PRACTICAL STEPS
1) Act quickly to stem all unnecessary expenditure and start bringing in cash.
2) Make a list of essentials. Involve all members of the family, so that they know how important it is to economise. Adult members of the family cannot take that foreign holiday. The children will have to wait for expensive new bikes or the latest video game. One desperate mum told National Debtline:
"The kids are always wanting things particularly for school. Teachers don't seem to realise, it's always a pound for this or that."
3) If there are debts, make a list and face up to the total without any fantasising about premium bond numbers coming up.

B) GET IT OUT INTO THE OPEN
This burden cannot be carried by one person alone. It is not disloyal to confide in someone – perhaps a doctor or close friend. Remember that one partner has got to stay sane, and that useful tips can often be collected from friends. Also, it is amazing how many other people are in the same boat, or have been in the past. It is easier to cope if you realise you are not on your own.

C) GET PROFESSIONAL HELP
Although it may not seem like a good idea to spend any more money, it may be sensible to seek professional advice. Perhaps the family's existing accountant is partly responsible for the mess. If so, ask someone whose business judgement you trust to recommend another. Never be afraid to ask a professional adviser such as a lawyer how much they charge per hour for their services, and to give a rough estimate of how much the problem will cost to sort out. Insist on being regularly billed for the service so that you can keep track of the cost. Professional advisers are not charitable agencies or Good Samaritans – they are running a business, and people in trouble are the source of their income.

D) THE LAW
If you are faced with clearing up the results of a failed business enterprise, do be aware that there are

potentially nasty legal consequences. For example, it is an offence to continue to obtain goods and services for a business, if you know that the debts already exceed any reasonable expectation of income. This is known as "trading insolvent". Personal bankruptcy if debts exceed £750 is an option to consider, because nowadays you are allowed to keep a reasonable amount (a roof over your head, your word processor, your telephone) to enable you to get re-started on earning a living, and the court proceedings, although unpleasant, will stop creditors from pestering you for unpaid bills.

BANKRUPTCY

Many small businesses rely on the family home as collateral to secure the business loan for working capital at the bank. This home is at risk if the bank forecloses on the loan, and forces the company into receivership or the owner into bankruptcy. However, if creditors are making life unpleasant, bankruptcy is a way of drawing a neat, firm line through the past and enabling you to make a fresh start.
What happens:
1) A business can go into voluntary liquidation, or a major creditor (usually the bank) may apply to put a business into liquidation.
2) A meeting of creditors is arranged and an official

receiver appointed. This is someone approved by the court to dispose of all the assets of a business in an orderly way, and distribute any proceeds fairly among those to whom the business owes money.

3) A half-way house which is becoming more common is called "administration" – a kind of intensive care for a business, during which the owners take a back seat voluntarily while an administrator (again, on behalf of creditors) tries to improve the situation while continuing to trade. If he succeeds, the business can be returned to its owners.

4) Yet another option is something called " voluntary arrangement". This is when someone who owes money gets his or her creditors together informally (i.e. not in front of a court), and agrees a scheme with them to repay the money owed.

REDUNDANCY

If someone is made redundant, it is worth remembering that it may be because the business in which he or she has been employed has foreseen the risk of "trading insolvent", and making staff redundant is the quickest way of avoiding this illegal state of affairs. However unpleasant and miserable redundancy is, it would be much more annoying to work for months, and then be told at the end that you weren't going to be paid because the company had run out of cash! Do not forget, if you or your partner has been asked to leave a job, and you feel that there was no good reason for it, there are steps you could consider taking to get compensation for wrongful dismissal. Also, being asked to take an enormous cut in salary or responsibilities might be something called "constructive dismissal" (meaning "as good as being sacked"). You might be able to claim compensation for that. Also, if a person is made redundant and discovers that another person has replaced them, they may be entitled to compensation.

Worst Scenario – WHAT HAPPENS AFTER THE CRISIS AND AFTER PROFESSIONAL HELP

1) BREAKDOWNS
People under stress can become depressed or even suicidal.

"Twice I had to go and find him sitting in his car on Beachy Head. It may seem obvious in retrospect that it was the classic 'cry for help' – but at the time it was terrifying."
(Rose)

Urge your partner to seek medical help or counselling if he is severely affected by the failure of his business or by losing his job. Keep an eye on your own health – you are not going to help the family if you fall in a heap as well.

"I started sleeping very badly, and once I fell asleep at the wheel of the car. I realised that I was on the edge myself – trying to cope with everything. I just had to let some things go for a while or I would have broken down completely."
(Georgina)

"I began to have back-ache, so I went to our doctor. He asked me some very simple questions and I simply burst into tears. It was only then that I realised how completely over-wrought I had become. He calmed me down and out it all poured. I felt so much better, just to have talked to someone about all my worries."
(Karen)

"When I worry, I eat. I just blew up like a balloon. Chocolate, cakes, biscuits. Sweet things were comforting, somehow. But then, of course, I got depressed with being overweight, so I went to the doctor and talking to him made me see I was trying to take on too much."
(Penny)

2) MARRIAGE STRAINS

Sadly, the stresses and strains of financial worry may exacerbate innate problems in the marriage.

The insights that a crisis brings are quite painful. They test people's feelings for each other.

"We didn't talk any more. I used to try and avoid him. If we tried to talk we only used to end up arguing."
(Rose)

Many couples in debt separate. Nearly all couples in this situation talk of splitting up, usually because one partner threatens to leave because they cannot cope with the financial pressures, or they blame the other for causing the financial problems.

CASE HISTORY: Sally
Sally F works full time. Her husband was made redundant in 1992. They have one child, a girl aged 12. After her husband lost his job, the Fs tried to manage on Sally's salary but they fell behind with their mortgage payments and credit card debts. Three of their creditors took action in the County court. Sally was suffering from asthma because of the pressure of trying to cope with the family's debts. She was very frightened that if her health continued to get much worse, she would have to take time off work, and as a result she feared she might also lose her job. She contacted Housing Debtline. This is part of the National Debtline service which offers a range of free confidential

advice on all aspects of indebtedness, including how to negotiate with creditors and reschedule debt. (See end for further details.) Sally told them: *"I feel at my wits' end with no one to turn to – we are in an awful and shameful mess."*

Fortunately there was an easy and affordable solution for the Fs. Sally and her husband applied for an Administration Order in their local County court. This added all their debts together, freezing interest and the court set an affordable payment until Mr F found work – which he finally did in March 1993.

Another woman in similar circumstances said:

"I feel as if a huge weight has been lifted off my shoulders. My depression is better. I am not shouting at the children for nothing, and our marriage is better than it has been for a long time. Without your help I wouldn't have known that the court would help us as well – and they were all very polite!"
(Theresa, 34, garment outworker)

Try and remember that getting divorced is expensive in every way – it takes its toll of emotion and cash. A huge proportion of single parents live below the poverty line. There is merit in keeping the marriage afloat. Partners have to remember to keep talking to each other – and listening. While there is talk there is hope. Often couples fight out the crisis together, but once this is over they find they can no longer stay together.

"I could put up with the failure of the business and the loss of the house, but when he went off and got a girl pregnant, I thought: this has got to stop. Even so, he kept coming back and begged me not to go through with the divorce, but by then I had had enough."
(Meriel, 55, SRN)

"After the crisis, I took a long hard look at my life, and thought: there must be a better way to live than this. And I have been lucky. Two years after the divorce, I met someone else – also divorced – and we married. Now I have someone who is not perfect, but at least I do not dread every phone call and every post in case there is a financial bombshell. I feel secure."
(Penny, 38, secretary).

If the crisis was one involving you as an anchor a break-up is more likely to occur. Other couples, having weathered the storm, find their relationship is stronger.

SILVER LINING

Financial problems can be very daunting. However, many successful business people have at least one failed enterprise behind them e.g. Michael Heseltine and Jeffrey Archer. Two people involved in painful change can try and see the situation as an opportunity rather than a threat.

"OK, his business failed, but looking back, we learned a hell of a lot. There were practical things, like over-trading, which is basically taking on too much work for too little reward. Dealing with the bank – we might have survived if we had warned the bank earlier, kept in closer touch. Credit – we will be far more careful another time about getting payment in, or extending credit to just anyone. A lot of clients let us down because they in turn were waiting to be paid. We were all caught in a vicious circle. Another time we will either grow more slowly or have a bigger drawing agreement with the bank. Cash is the name of the game at the end of the day. We had terrible arguments and sleepless nights, and there are bruises still. But, no, I wouldn't rule out trying again some day."
(Rose)

Adversity strengthens family ties. The family that has faced economic collapse together and survived

161

to tell the tale has a tremendous bond of solidarity behind it. One day you may all be able to look back on lessons learned, friendships tested and love growing alongside of loyalty to your partner in trouble.

"J had these really dreadful foreign business partners. That was a big part of the problem. We depended on them for the goods we were trading in. The other day we heard they had set up a sandwich bar together. It was so incongruous. We were able to laugh for the first time about the whole grisly experience. You laugh far more about the really bad things than about when things went well."
(Bridget)

"All I remember when Mum was driving us away from our house – it had been repossessed – she said: 'This is what they call a character building experience.' At the time, I thought: what a weird thing to say. But she was right. I grew up that day. A lot of things that had been bothering me just faded into insignificance. The world didn't come to an end. Life went on. I'm determined to get on now, whereas I couldn't really have cared less before."
(Adam, 19, history student).

162

APPENDICES

APPENDICES

1. WORDS OF COMFORT

The following Christian text has helped many partners at difficult times:

"One night a woman had a dream. She dreamed she was walking along the beach with the Lord. Across the sky flashed scenes from her life. On each scene, she noticed two sets of footprints in the sand: one belonging to her and the other to the Lord.

When the last scene of her life flashed before her, she looked back at the footprints in the sand. She noticed that many times along the path of her life there was only one set of footprints. She also noticed that it happened at the very lowest and saddest times in her life.

This really bothered her and she questioned the Lord about it. 'Lord, you said that once I decided to follow you, you'd walk with me all the way. But I have noticed that during the most troublesome times in my life, there is only one set of footprints. I don't understand why when I needed you most you would leave me.'

The Lord replied, 'My precious, precious child, I love you and I would never leave you. During your times of trial and suffering when you see only one set of footprints, it was then that I carried you'."

This text, too, has comforted many carers:

"Death is nothing at all . . . I have only slipped away into the next room . . . I am I and you are you . . . whatever we were to each other that we are still. Call me by my old familiar name, speak to me in the easy way which you always used. Put no difference into your tone; wear no forced air of solemnity or sorrow. Laugh as we always laughed at the little jokes we enjoyed together. Play, smile, think of me, pray for me. Let my name be ever the household word it ever was. Let it be spoken without effect, without the ghost of a shadow on it. Life means all that it ever meant. It is the same as it ever was; there is absolutely unbroken continuity. What is this death, but a negligible accident. Why should I be out of mind because I am out of sight? I am but waiting for you, for an interval, somewhere very near just around the corner . . . All is well."
(Henry Scott Holland)

Fatalists might like to memorise Arthur Marshall's dictum:

"Expect the worst, hope for the best and take what comes."

Or ponder this:

"There are worse things than death."

On looking up at a tree:

"As I watched the imperceptible trembling of its leaves against an endless sky, I was overcome by a sensation that is difficult to describe: all at once, I seemed to rise above all the coordinates of my momentary existence in the world into a kind of state outside time in which all the beautiful things I had ever seen and experienced existed in a total 'co-present'; I felt a sense of reconciliation, indeed of an almost gentle consent to the inevitable course of things as revealed to me now, and this combined with a carefree determination to face what had to be faced . . . I was flooded with a sense of ultimate happiness and harmony with the world and myself, with that moment, with all the moments I could call up, and with everything invisible that lies behind it and which has meaning."
(Vaclav Havel in his *Letters to Olga* (his wife) from prison, June 1982)

On putting things into perspective:

"There are two equal and eternal ways of looking at this twilight world of ours; we may see it as the twilight of evening or the twilight of morning; we may think of

anything, down to a fallen acorn, as a descendant or an ancestor. There are times when we are crushed, not so much with the load of evil as with the load of the goodness of humanity, when we feel that we are nothing but the inheritors of a humiliating splendour. But there are other times when everything seems primitive, when the ancient stars are only sparks blown from a boy's bonfire, when the whole earth seems so young and experimental that even the white hair of the aged, in the fine biblical phrase, is like almond-trees that blossom, like the white hawthorn grown in May."
(G.K. Chesterton, from his essay 'A Defence of Nonsense'

On self-sufficiency:

"The sooner we realise our fate lies in ourselves and not in the stars, so much the better for us."
(Axel Munthe, *The Story of San Michele*)

On the consolation of nature:

"She never found comfort
When a friend told her
To weep her pain away
And offered a shoulder

But a thin tan lizard
Lying on a boulder,

Indifferent and delicate,
Greatly consoled her"
(Marie de L. Welch)

"I said to my soul, be still, and wait without hope
For hope would be hope for the wrong thing; wait
without love
For love would be love of the wrong thing; there is
yet faith
But the faith and the love and the hope are all in the
waiting.
Wait without thought, for you are not ready for the
thought:
So the darkness shall be the light, and the stillness
the dancing."
(T.S. Eliot, *East Coker Four Quartets*)

On acceptance:

"Give us the courage to change those things that
can be changed, the patience to bear those things
that cannot be changed, and the wisdom to know
the difference."
(Reinhold Niebuhr)

On forgiveness:

"Mutual forgiveness of each vice
These are the Gates of Paradise"
(William Blake)

2. FACTFILE

ALCOHOL ABUSE:

ACCEPT,
724 Fulham Rd.,
London SW6 5SE
071-371 7477.
It offers counselling, information and advice for people who have problems with drink. Can give you information on local organisations which can be of help (ACCEPT only has one branch)

Al-Anon for Relatives,
61 Great Dover Street,
London SE1 4YF.
Tel: 071 403 0888.
Provides free, friendly, confidential advice for the families and friends of problem drinkers.

Alcohol Concern,
275 Grays Inn Road,
London WC1X 8QF.
Tel: 071 833 3471.
Carries out research on alcohol and health. Visits by appointment only.

ALCOHOL/DRUG ABUSE:

Charter Clinic,
1–5 Radnor Walk,
London SW3 4PB.
Tel: 071 351 1272.
Also at 11–19 Lisson Grove,
London NW1 6SH.
Tel: 071 258 3828.
For alcohol/drug and stress-related problems.

CoDa, (Co-Dependents Anonymous),
PO BOX 1292,
London N4 2XX.
Tel: 071 409 0029.
For people who feel they may be co-dependent on
a drug user or problem drinker.

ALZHEIMER'S DISEASE:

Alzheimer's Disease Society, (Headquarters)
National Office,
Gordon House,
10 Greencoat Place,
London SW1P 1PH.
Tel: 071 306 0606/071 306 0833.
The society will supply lists of regional development
officers and research specialists all over Britain.

Have the Men Had Enough? Margaret Forster (Penguin, £5.99). A novel with an Alzheimer's theme.

COUNSELLING:

British Association for Counselling,
37a Sheep Street,
Rugby,
Warwickshire, CV21 3BX.
Tel: 0788 578328.

FWA (The Family Welfare Association)
501 Kingsland Rd,
London E8 4AU
Tel: 081 969 3825.
This provides a social work and counselling service for individuals, couples and families.

The Samaritans is a nationwide organisation that offers counsellors who are specially trained and will listen in strict confidence to people in crisis. Local numbers available in all regional phone directories.

DRUG ABUSE:

Adfam National,
1st Floor,
Chapel House,
18 Hatton Place,
London EC1N
Tel: 071-405 3923
For families and friends of drug users.

The Institute for the Study of Drug Dependence,
1 Hatton Place,
London EC1N 8ND.
Tel: 071 430 1991 or 071 430 1993.
For information and up-to-date research and books.

NCVO National Council for Voluntary Organisations,
Regents Wharf,
All Saints Street,
London N1 9RL.
Tel: 071 713 6161.
Offers skilled help in setting up self-help group for families and friends of drug users.

Release,
388 Old Street,
London EC1V 9LT.
Tel: 071 729 9904.
Helpline offering legal advice and information.

SCODA (Standing Conference on Drug Abuse),
1–4 Hatton Place,
London EC1N 8ND.
Will provide a complete list of services for drug users, their relatives and friends in your area.

FINANCIAL ADVICE AND BENEFITS:

Free copies of DSS booklets describing changes in income support, social security benefits and community care changes in April 1993 can be obtained from:
Health Publications Unit,
Heywood Stores,
No2 Site,
Manchester Road,
Heywood,
Lancashire PL10 2PZ.
Tel: 0800 666 555 Freeline Social Security.

Lloyd's Hardship Fund,
John Thompson,
Lloyd's, Dock Road,
Chatham,
Kent ME4 4TU.
Tel: 0634 882460.

National Association of Citizens Advice Bureaux,
136–144 City Road,
London EC1V.
Tel: 071 833 2181.
This will give you the address of your local CAB, which can explain benefits to which you are entitled.

National Debtline for Debt Counselling,
Birmingham Settlement,
318 Summer Lane,
Birmingham B19 3RL.
Tel: 021 359 3562 or (housing) 021 359 8501.

Redundancy: Coping and Bouncing Back Jenny Woolf (Piccadilly Press, £6.99). Everything you need to know about the practical and emotional aspects of redundancy.

HOMEOPATHY:

Homeopathic Medical Association,
6 Livingstone Road,
Gravesend,
Kent DA12 5DZ.
Tel: 0474 560336.

Institute for Complementary Medicine,
PO Box 194,
London SE16 1QZ.
Tel: 071 237 5165.

Society of Homeopaths,
2 Artisan Road,
Northampton NN1 4HU.
Tel: 0604 21400.

MARRIAGE PROBLEMS:

Relate, (National Headquarters)
Herbert Gray College,
Little Church Street,
Rugby,
Warwickshire CV21 7LB.
Tel: 0788 573241.

Solicitors Family Law Association will provide a list of lawyers in your area who are committed to a conciliatory rather than litigious approach to family breakdown. Free booklet available from:
Mary l'anson,
Permanent Secretary,
SFLA,
PO Box 302,
Keston,
Kent BR2 6EZ.
Tel: 0689 850227.

The Divorce Handbook, Fiona Shackleton and Olivia Timbs (Thorsons in association with Farrer & Co., £6.99).

MENTAL ILLNESS:

MIND,
(Headquarters) 22 Harley Street,
London W1.
Tel: 071 637 0741.
It can offer experience and understanding of mental health problems and will advise and provide information on local representatives.

STRESS:
The Centre for Stress Management,
156 Westcombe Hill,
Blackheath,
London SE3 7DH.
Tel: 081 293 4114.
Has videos and books and runs courses on stress
management and counselling based on a broad
spectrum cognitive-behavioural approach.

Coping with Stress,
Dave MacDonald (ISDD, £4.00).
Written especially for those working with drug
addicts, but also a very good self-help guide. Con-
tains a stress diary and stress identification chart.

Count to Ten and Think Again,
A free leaflet containing tips to beat stress, available
from NSPCC. Tel: 0800 800 500.
Gives practical advice for parents of children of all
ages and provides addresses of helpful organisations.

PHYSICAL DISABILITY/ILLNESS:

Disability Information and Advice Service,
16 Dalston Lane,
London E8.
Tel: 071 275 8485.

There are many individual organisations catering for specific disabilities/illnesses. Their addresses can be found in the phone book.

WORKING WOMEN
The Women Returners Network Development Officer,
100 Park Village East,
London, NW1.
Tel: 071 226 4026.
This gives information on jobshare, part-time and term-time work.

The Working Parents Handbook
(Working Mothers Association, £4.50 inc., p&p).
Available from WMA,
77 Holloway Road,
London N7 8JZ.
Tel: 071-700 5771.
This is full of excellent advice and reassurance and useful information, names and addresses.

3. INDEX

Appendices – Index